From the Riddle Me Collection
Volume One: A Stone's Throw

Jack Brutus Penny was born in September 1986 in London, England, and grew up in the north London area. At school, under the advice of his English teacher, he was tested and diagnosed with dyslexia. Not held back, after graduating with a degree is Psychology, he moved to Kanagawa, Japan. Since then he has had a variety of jobs, including: English lecturer, private interpreter, free-lance graphic designer, writer and illustrator. His works, all in the nonsense genre, include volumes from the *Riddle Me Collection*, *In Truth Stories* (in editing), and *The Allegaurus* (in editing).

10263780

Volume One: A Stone's Throw

Jack Brutus Penny

Copyright © 2016 by Jack Brutus Penny
All rights reserved. This book or any portion thereof may not be reproduced or used in any manner whatsoever without the express written permission of the publisher except for the use of brief quotations in a book review.

JBP Publishing
First Printing, 2016

ISBN 978-4-908906-00-8

www.jackbrutuspenny.com

From the Riddle Me Collection

To whom this book is dedicated.

1.

I am a flower barely bloomed,
Only when young am I consumed
In Arab beds with bulbous leg,
That lays a single golden egg,
My sapid yield is in my heart,
The rest of me is choke and tart.

CONTENTS

INTRODUCTION 1

RIDDLES 4
The Crude Lad 7
My girlfriend pops her knuckles 13
My Misstep 32
Speck of Light Lustre 41
The Mischievous Stripling 51
From My Girlfriend's Collection 63
Tongue Twisting 69
The African Lynx 71
It's Pie 73

ANSWERS 80

EXPLANATIONS 82
Illustration I 84
Illustration II 89
Illustration III 91
Illustration IV 94
Illustration V 100
Illustration VI 105
Look Mum 109
Illustration VII 118
Illustration VIII 121
Illustration IX 126
You're Here 128
Illustration X 132
Illustration XI 143
Illustration XII 148
Illustration XIII 161

Introduction

The Riddle Me Collection is a collection of riddles self-proclaimed and entirely unsupported to be some of the hardest in the English language. Riddles typically fall into two categories: the enigmas, the allegorical metaphors of Plato's cave of shadows, and the conundra, the playful puns that allow the river to run though it has no legs, but stops the river from ever sleeping or talking though it has a bed and a mouth each. However, though the riddles in this collection may play with enigma and conundra, an entirely new nature is given: riddles that rely on language. Well clearly that statement is past absurd, so let's expand it - riddles that rely on the idiomatic, expressive, proverbial and etymological use of the English language.

If I am slow I may be a poke, or if I'm not I may be sure. If I am bold I may be brass, favoured by fortune, or made to venture. What is up may not be up but in fact belted and so quiet, while what is down may be brought, at least by a peg or two.

So in this book find two intentions, implicitly not again marked, or unremarked other than here: to stretch the tongue within your intellect, and to see how nonsense a thoughtful question can be.

The Riddle Me Collection presents riddles, some rather difficult and others unreasonably so. As such, before you begin, allow me to explain how the riddles might be tackled. There are two steps to each riddle, the first is solving it, and the second explaining it. Each riddle buries an inkling, the collective of references, clues and hints, within it. If you can latch on to one reference and test it against the rest, you'll either come to the conclusion, or the conclusion that you shan't. Whichever way, even once you've found and or checked the answer, you still haven't understood the inkling in its entirety. Go back then, and try to find each reference to that answer, before turning to the explanations provided.

Riddle two is an easier one to address, as it doesn't care for etiquette or formalities.

2.

I spin, and round and round not dizzy,
Like a spinning top and busy
Turning, be at me resigned
To never first, always behind,
But careful, dreams will bring your death they weep;
At me don't fall asleep.

I spin, and round and round not dizzy, well what is apparently being described is something that spins but doesn't feel dizzy. Be at me resigned notes that people are said to be at it, while to never first, always behind betokens whomever is at it must be behind it. If you've an idea that seems to fit these clues then check the answer page, which you'll find is a problem in itself. Then return here to try to explain each of the lines more assertively. Once all is said and done, check the explanation for the trickier references.

Riddle three is a little tougher, though neither a pill nor something to swallow, whether tree, barn, or common house.

3.

I have no mouth but there a spoke
Put in me, on such words I choke,
See fortune's me, luck's where it lands,
I come in two and four me bands,
But where a two and one more nuisance spurred;
A third.

What spoke with no mouth? What is owned by fortune? What is a nuisance when three? Again if you've an assured idea, check the answer, return to explain it, then review the explanations.

Riddles

4.

I pose though no one takes a picture,
Lead to science or to scripture,
Both are out of me it seems
I'll haunt you in your wake and dreams
I'm smart, there's nothing else I'd be,
Move on, just love; pop me.

5.

I'm quiet as a mouse backstage,
Till curtains up and play-writes rage,
I carry secrets cloaked akin,
But change when on east porcelain,
The harder you do coax me dear,
The more I disappear.

6.

I'm slender, one princess no pea,
And pure, how things look good on me,
You seek me? Fine, I'll leave a trail
Put cage to me; tell my tale
Clean but even if I'm dirtied, gosh;
I won't dare wash.

7.

What's up but down and left but right?
A raven and a desk to write
A language only talked in tongues,
In squirming insects covered, bung,
I drive you mad, insane, green eggs and ham;
I'm what I am.

8.

A shell that inside keeps a pearl
That from which all the world unfurls,
That delicate it needs a case,
So in this hollow chamber placed,
My walls are hard as cobbled brick,
It shan't get through; my walls are thick.

9.

You come to see me, to my face
You scream and shout and jump and brace
Yourself, in me you throw your hands
Up, hide your eyes and crouch or stand
Up, behave or it's straight to bed and still hungry;
You little me.

10.

Wine, salt and I, we bare your toil,
Rejoice! Mark a dastard foil,
Look the same as shreds left hung
But sound to some as layers strung,
In barrage, comes your core with ease
And bursts you into mes.

The Crude Lad

There once was a frantic crude lad,
Frenzied, foolhardy, and mad.
He flooded his room,
And in swimming costume,
Sat there with a yellowtail scad.

11.

I can't be short, but can be long,
I'm it! Accept and head out strong,
You can't buy me but value check
I'm never full but stuffed, bedecked
With one tall mountain, upwards stretching crane;
It's just as plain.

12.

I'm made by someone madly raving,
Sit atop the sop, I'm craving
Spectacle, applause and cheers,
From me I'll pull on someone's ears,
So off I come, the job well done, surprising feat;
Myself I'll eat!

13.

I'm fixed in shape but bend with ease,
Though I won't break with the same breeze,
The wind would pick me up, that light
I tumble but I won't take flight,
I'll bind a leaf, combined a leaf,
Remove me and the bind is brief.

14.

At the ball, just mee, let's dance;
Hear me and all the whistles prance
There aft you want to go again?
Give them a me and just say when
Not sour, sweet, no taste but heavens;
Oranges and lemons.

15.

I'm up, so keep me there old chap,
Though I point down by some mishap,
So use me, wag me, now with chums
And take it on me, what e'er comes
Just drink it up like cups of tea, let's laugh and be merry,
Me me.

16.

Give me to me, I'm everywhere,
In corn and wheat, the trees, take care!
From elephants to mice it's clear
In pigs, though that's a mess I fear
A snow-topped range from me to me,
Though only when happy.

17.

I come in many types they say,
So eyes fix straight to me and stay
But note, I take no shoe, just cotton
Seems I like to hit, how rotten!
Mind, don't prod me, push or barge;
I'm positive, I'll charge.

18.

I'm hard to see, you know I'm there,
You know what's fore, aft, everywhere
Around, and let me crack my mouth
Comes heavy breaths from north and south,
I'm bought, though spend none, take none home, not free,
But opportunity.

19.

A hundred teeth but not one tongue
That scrape wherever they are flung,
That till no soil, grasses rake
And shake the grass for shaking's sake,
In fact inane, all efforts felled by draft;
You're just as daft.

20.

I am a trick, I'm all but smoke
And to a lick I'll copy folk,
I have your nose, your mouth I took,
I stole both of your eyes, just look!
I see where snow has settled merrily, I'm on the wall;
So call.

21.

A heath, where on a cliff I wave,
And out of place I angry rave,
Don't startle me, I'll raise and in
The moment, cross, confound chagrin,
So cut me, crush me, burn; where e'er I sit,
I don't know what to do, I'm split.

22.

I'm holed and tied down 'gainst my will,
So I hold back, a hole I fill,
I'm pushed and down in lines I run,
But when I'm lined, at last not done,
So hit me right and make it true,
I'll make a brighter you.

23.

A cloud, I gaily float around,
Until I fall sheer to the ground
And die, in me you're strongly fixed,
Won't change so pull me up betwixt
Your eyes, the world, you've had enough, this icy storm;
Here's safe and warm.

24.

I end the branch and hold it tight,
With you I change, your length and height,
I'm on you, though you feel me naught
And off-me, do without a thought,
If I won't close, no hex or jinx,
You need a couple links.

My girlfriend pops her knuckles

My girlfriend pops her knuckles,
pop-pop, there they go,
Whilst I venture to my happy place;
Vineyards in south Bordeaux,
The grapes yield old from distant Thrace
Through which I walk as wrapped in lace
in vines that softly coup de grace
and smells that sing and dance, embrace
to bottle, cork, and lay in place
for years they sit, the tastes encase,
until the mauve hearts beat and race
the bottles lifted, give breathing space
Set down in the Chateaux,
I lift them up, stopper to face, but,
pop-pop, there they go.

25.

I'm half, not underhand, I slip
In through myself, around and dip,
Go figure, hate that Great old sword
That challenge cut of its accord,
But take two lovers, husband bride,
With which a cord is tied.

26.

The icing on the cake I show
The main event, around I glow,
I word it special ways, and then
Because of me you're caught and penned,
You think what's in me's good or bad? Then find
A me of mind.

27.

I'm run and through it all you'll find
The things you'd by chance left behind,
I'm flat, though it's my shape that matters
Light, though through that beach it clatters
Silent brushed each dental edge, hedge sheath;
How fine my teeth.

28.

Today I'm here but gone the next,
Nights disappear, ties loosened, vexed
From greater beasts, when one I plumb,
When two from different critters come,
I'm chic and in or stale and out,
And from the end I sprout.

29.

I carpet cover, welcome in,
And move much but not far I've been,
I'm with a cheek quite farcical,
And forcibly an arsenal
I writhe and squirm and from me come,
But nothing from those dumb.

30.

You love to get me, I come baring
From far places, Greek beware!
String gab together, weave a spell
For with me given you speak well
With hands and heart make art of me,
Redundantly I'm free.

31.

First you meet to make a bloody
Big boat only for you, buddy
Up, sometimes a rocky ride
Sometimes more green when hedges hide
An end that drifts apart but starts up cruelly;
You strike me.

32.

The tips of cues made from my buds
Picked in the farms, the righteous floods
Of politics will rid the trade till gone
On, see it's time to get me on
So bless that child, bless her soul that shines;
Her socks of mine.

33.

Punch, I was a boxer briefly,
Fancy me, a smarty chiefly
Running 'round all hither-thither
Ants fill me and stop your dither
Dally, folly frolic all 'round town;
You're caught me down.

34.

Put me in arms, put me in neck,
I am a collarbone gone trek,
I like the powerful and rich,
On them I'm me, get some for which
My burdens change and pull each day,
So differently I weigh.

35.

I'm hello, maybe twice, and blow,
I float, I'm clearly caught, I know
I happen but I'll tell you not,
I'll bring you life and breath, last shot;
Last chance to see, farewell and me, don't cry;
For I'm goodbye.

36.

I'm dizzy, all I do is turn,
You lose an eye and then you learn
To decorate me roses red,
Then put them in another's bed,
But that's some me right there, risky you sprung,
I ate your tongue.

37.

From whence a worm the tendrils spout
A mothball woven, flattened out
And smooth, it softly falls on skin,
Won't break though nearly paper thin
And light, but find a sow's ear cursed, adverse
To make my purse.

38.

I march in pairs, come two by two,
And four a kind I quickly grew
At first I cut, and then I bark,
The third and forth both bury. Hark!
This cave I broach is caving in,
Still in the dark, I grin.

39.

I me along, both smooth and fast
Follow my track, retrace my past,
I past someone, they see me by,
In fact, as I go up I fly!
You moan, when you're with me you're still I move, you move I sit;
Me it!

40.

The cave door opens, winds rush in
And echo, whir and moan a din,
The jagged rocks above all rumple,
Then to rest back where they crumpled,
Hollows near, the cracks and caves,
Now through the same wind waves.

41.

Hated, loved, or in between,
I stain, a spot but spotless-clean,
I find what's open, not what's closed
Once set, to move I'm indisposed
And sometimes this relentless comer
Hides in winter, plays in summer.

42.

I'm on your hand, my voice I threw;
I'm on your ear, and in it too,
Less planets, Mercury, the Sun,
Venus, Earth, Mars; show-off and run
And when you're sure your love's not spent, present;
I'm busy sent.

43.

I'm cold and hard, it's easy that
Way, give me credit, I'll talk, chat,
Say problems flowing? I won't be
Made? It takes time, I am heavy
Weighed all the options? Placed a bet? Came tops? Chinchin! You win!
I'm in.

44.

A row of numbers, doubles made,
Though one foul pair doth masquerade,
I'm green, though not from envy dabble;
Rest, don't lift me feet up, babble
On, for if you work too hard; ungrown,
You'll leave me bone.

45.

Iron me, but full of air,
I'm stronger with each bond, I share
My nerves, you take them, keep them close,
show them and show my strength the most
Against, so me your heart and see you can,
As I own Superman.

46.

I'm fit, compare all else to me,
Takes time to wear me, out foxy,
Get out! A spider-less three legs,
Put in your spiny dexterous pegs,
You think you're tough? You think I won't stand on my own? I'm soft?
I'm off!

47.

As strong as is the strongest man,
The weakest yet undo me can,
My gold is dubious but settled
Good and bad; a nettled petal
Grant, I promise, agree all,
And up and down I sprawl.

48.

Work harder, dip your elbow in
And put it on their palms, a sin
That makes it all go faster, right!
That's why the thunder lost to light!
Though some by hand may place it, shape it, there;
Best wash your hair.

49.

My man, you'll catch your death of heat,
So here's a carrot not to eat,
Grab cotton pads and caste them out,
You're under me? Abundant drought!
No school or work, a call to play, away!
For it's my day.

50.

A means to bake a cake; just sing,
A way to downward clean a thing,
A way, still down, to make it flat,
A postman with a two-toned cat,
A manner calms or says well done and thwack,
On head and back.

51.

A knot once tied that's never un-
A hole that lies in plateau one,
A fasten you can't fasten up,
A fasten made when you're a pup,
Another name a great sea boat,
Of many things I gloat.

52.

Lean on me when you're not strong,
I'll be there if where I belong,
Not wooden leg, but backed by wood,
No hand where one would think I should,
Though not the same, you've one of me; same crop,
Which you then put on top.

53.

I'm part of you not always there,
In me chance dropped a strange affair;
Now me it up and make the most
In luxury of mine you boast;
Well done old boy! Superb! Kudos! Your victory!
Go take a me.

54.

No me, you hate to hear us all,
Or if, just do the job you bawl,
Though wait however they all plea
Defy, one shan't comply all me,
I'm gone, farewell, adieu to you, I'm rotten;
Not forgotten.

55.

I'm made of what I am and hold
In me what keeps my errors scold
And put me like a cat on top,
Where music beats but my ears bop;
Alors, mon dieu! The clue's a key;
The case afoot, so send meme.

56.

A lidless box, a faceless head,
I'm kicked not hurt, but now you're dead,
All left a hole my dearest Liza,
From which flows an upturned geyser,
Now you're gone, though most the points you missed
Upon my list.

57.

I'm mad? Well if so made by you!
The Hare in Spring now sprung anew
Brew made from me, so me to it
And fill the flask spilt, I can't sit,
Can't stop, I'm bound to change, too long the same I'm vexed;
What channel's next?

58.

'My me!' I said, you took offence
And sabotage, shot me in, whence
Was I alone put in the grave
And learnt when meeting best behave;
Make sure that right not wrong, the first has gone,
You get off on.

59.

Not open, best it's hid away,
So under me and leave me lay,
Not you, for only kings unfurl
For queens, lords, ladies, dukes and earls
For street rats, magic, take a seat;
See me move with no feet.

60.

I come and in a moment gone
But feel as if I linger on
My mark an insult, face head-first
But can't? To wrist or else far worse;
I'm quick and dash, though carelessly,
That's me.

61.

I come in two that can be changed,
Though never swapped or rearranged,
The first is dropped and then we wait,
The other's coming though it's late,
Ah here it is, you mind your edge though soft cow skin;
You're one me in.

62.

I'm full though didn't eat it all,
If not then all may fall to squall,
You heard me, then you have me known,
So leave, farewell, well me alone,
Speak to myself; can't 'thank you' me, decry
That I is I!

63.

I thread and squirm through every hoop
And fast I stop the land from drooping
Down, hush now, me up! And just admit,
'twas low a blow below me hit,
Keep secrets, know your stuff, thoust wily thee;
Kept under me.

64.

You want me but you rarely need,
With me you couldn't have agreed,
You bite me though you wish you'd not,
Despite, I make a merry lot,
So plead sir, ask for me, but don't dare press;
It's me or less.

65.

My colours change, now purple, blue or green,
They fade where once so clearly seen
A scene that if just once more hit,
Is famed to bring me back a bit,
Despite this I'm quite sensitive and such;
With me you'll need a lighter touch.

66.

I make a pile burnt, so called,
I make the box around, so walled,
I'm not the best though record keep,
Of data stacks and dates in heaps,
I'm good with beats, and counting, sing;
That I'm a rhythmic thing.

67.

I tipper-tap and dance with glee,
No mind but what a clever me!
You see me come and all you stop;
I'm up, you're still until I drop,
I've many types in many forms made good, I should
Be wood.

68.

The canvas ripped, it grows more round,
And what you didn't seek is found
And opened up, it might be old,
Retell a story not since told,
Get over quick, that's in a lick. You're prime?
Just give it time.

69.

You're me a sore, a poor excuse,
Let bygones be, I'm for a truce,
But stubborn see, and temperate,
I'll never come, won't budge a foot,
And never made, don't kid; and I'm sorry,
But is not me.

70.

I think but far more casual
I work; see my effects enthral,
Enthralled, beguiled, seven were
Great tombs and gardens, lighthouse, spur
On me, and one day you'll succeed you dunce,
Just hit it once.

71.

I've got four arms all fixed to bend
A problem? I'll that problem mend,
You greet me with a smiling face,
And though I'm strong I leave no trace,
The strongest is not lion, horse, not bull, not theirs;
No, it's the Bear's.

72.

In me you fly up to the sun
And fall, keep falling, get up! Run!
In me you're chased but never caught,
In me you're lost in your own thoughts,
But never will you ever really be, though pray and plea,
Quite in your me!

73.

Just look up then and follow me,
How could you? You're not bird nor bee,
You sail the sea with pins that pull
Until you find the true me full
Of one-day-years, and six month nights
Illuminating with my lights.

74.

I'm rare and inexplicable,
But rarely seen despicable
Me, for I'm good the work of Gods
Work me, perform and break the odds,
I'll feed with naught, make land of sea,
As unpredictable as me.

75.

I hide, you'll never see past me,
I'm wide, as both the land and sea,
I never move but sit aglow,
You aim but never reach me though,
And soon on me you'll find your grander dreams are near to hand;
One I'll expand.

76.

I wake first as it's brighter here,
My place is far or middle, fear
The other's over there replete
Between us we shall never meet
Wherever then you go, know home's easy,
But I am me.

77.

I'm loose both physical and ethic,
Pull the ropes! The sails tear quick
Cut some me, the job's not bad,
All that's me's picked up, just be glad
Enough, I'm tired, ah-hum, it's that time already? Well I, cough,
I'm off.

78.

I'm cut but know that is the best,
The newest, end of where I rest,
I perch and anxious listen from my seat,
You have a me so have them beat
The drum and clap, I'm at an end
Of there append.

79.

It's all gone bad to me it's come
And with the birds and their hum-drum
I'm warmer though it more depends
On where you're standing now my friends,
And by-and-by I'm only I
Because of how the paper lies.

80.

I'm guilty though I did no wrong,
When I was up, I'd fallen strong,
You grazed the surface, scarred quite drastic,
I'm the light you lost fantastic,
Taken down a path of words; story, that's me
Of memory.

My Misstep

My erstwhile misstep first took me
To the venomous hive of a bee.
It stung me all over,
Till green as a clover
To the Biloba tree I did flee.

The maidenhair Biloba fruit
Was said to make mad-men astute
Dribbling its juice
As if poured from a sluice
Made me see naught but a newt.

The newt told me 'be not afraid!'
With the look of a livid tirade
But heeding no warning
I bid him 'Good morning'
And made for the jade promenade.

The glistening glimmering green
To-a-tea matched m' pelt in its sheen
With emerald skin
I blended right in
So that surely I couldn't be seen.

But seen, it turned out, that I was,
By a bellowing bear and his paws
Zealously lifted
With beady eyes shifted
To sweep this sweet-pea to his jaws.

But down the hedge-way I did hurtle
Till I tripped on a mound of moist murtle.
It opened its bill
With a deafening shrill
And cried, 'Dost you defy a dove turtle?'

To the dove turtle my story I'd share
Of the bee, tree, the newt and the bear.
He lent all a'bent
As he listened intent.
'I'll start at the misstep affair.'

81.

On boards a mouldy rolling-pin afar;
I'm kept submerged in rooms ajar,
Of glass or chequered high glass stacks
Of thirty holy Mary's axe,
Oh dear, good gosh, rhymes absentee;
I'm in a pretty family.

82.

I'm small but with long history,
Just close your eyes and think of me;
Of ancient feet and burning bows,
Where lines are queues and rows just rows
And rowers go, smart sweat on hands, they band;
To seas of angles land.

83.

I'm all, I'm yours, so take my pearl;
I'm given to you, every girl
And boy will know you told me so,
Though not enough? I'm double! Oh,
My difference is but everything, claw cling,
You're on me; king.

84.

Go me, pet shops to other lands,
My life sings popular in bands
Of men with holsters, hats and guns
That ride into the setting sun
That sets right here so don't ride far
Or else you'll miss just where we are.

85.

You see me go and see me come,
Can't ever hold or touch, the sum
Of me the same though long or short,
Won't give my time to those your sort,
Except to say thank you, through your tirade,
My me you made.

86.

I'm done to many things, how queer;
Backwards and over that one's ear,
To rules and laws that govern lands
In futures may those falling sands
Be me-d and out of shape, insane; to sylums bound
The me-go-round.

87.

I can't be changed, not sold nor bought,
From me though most your lessons taught
Your troubles seemed so far to be
Recalled, cryptic, mixed; stay reedy.
Not dim, not born to me, you're in your prime;
A ye olde time.

88.

I'm hard, so try to make me light,
I'm in the day but gone at night
And grunt, I'm tiring, don't bark
But like a dog and not the lark
Around I'll stay until I'm done, the battle beat;
I'm like a treat.

89.

I know your name, your age, your face,
In fact, I know your town, birthplace,
I know some details you forget,
I'm more like you than you I bet
When face-to-face, they don't know you,
They ask to see, but guess who? Me!

90.

I sit outside come sun or rain,
In gardens, parks, town streets or lanes
And to your purpose me be on,
But on me, left to crowds anon,
You judge your progress on my back, my legs stand stark, so hark,
I set my mark.

91.

You know the joke and I was there,
What's monotone and coloured? Stare
A moment, see my woven arts;
I'm like the onion, many parts,
I see the dead and speak of loss,
I break but stay the same across.

92.

Of several brothers I am one,
Though which, I change when each one's done
So here I am, the next I'm gone,
So fleetingly I'm lost, a con
To think to live as I, the moment be
To now I'm me.

93.

I am, though act as if I'm not,
I'm clearly coming, never spot
Me, never see, I'll never be
So panic, you can't ever flee;
So let us eat, drink merrily, and why?
For me we die.

94.

First I am tender, seeming tripe,
But grow until I'm good and ripe,
Now pretty people follow and
I act dependent on my stand,
But careful tread, and mind your words; I know, but honestly
Best don't ask me!

95.

A halo round of yellows, pinks,
Of blues and whites and with a blink
I'm here where once I curled up warm,
Now warmer in the sun, I form
Like tears that slowly tumble weep
As everything goes back to sleep.

96.

Bakers six-point-five the dozen,
More a distant kind of cousin,
See then how my other lives
As with my heart dull efforts give,
For you've but heard a part, a wee
Bit that's not even me.

97.

You change your style where upon
You take me off or put me on,
In donkey's measured and aghast
I'm light, so far I sure move fast;
Don't run, won't skip or jump a heap,
But sometimes leap.

98.

Hop to it, though I'm short a jump
Rope me in, loaf me a step bump
The class, I'm out now lost the chance;
Less in the run, I'm more a prance,
So startled, starts your heart and happy feet;
Do me a beat.

99.

Before the face, my little friend,
There was my little head, this bending
Box that soon would open, nod,
The best as if from the same pod
And see that trouble's coming, with a snip,
Give it a nip.

100.

Think hard, I'll me to mind
And forever hope you will find
I'm once an orbit, life is fresh
And I'll to life, no chicken crèche,
In bed I spiral up and push, push off that lazy sheet;
From me to feet.

Speck of Light Lustre

Bawl, the wind wails,
O, would beat down a bluster,
Kick up the chrome leaves,
Not a speck of light lustre.

The kingbird accords,
Not a tyrant flycatcher,
But jostled upon
As would feather-faint stature.

The forest it yawps,
Out! Vain thrashing about,
Could but weep off skin
Accept these alms doled devout.

The bud that breaks soil
Tucks its head fast back under,
Lest tempestuous gail
Hails seeking its plunder.

As with swarthy storms,
As great shore ridges weather,
They tire soon out,
O, make fast stalwart tether.

Bawl, the wind wails,
O, would beat down a bluster,
Then settle chrome leaves,
Sneak back speck of light lustre.

101.

How old are you? You've met that sum
And as the birds and bees calm, comes
The Swallow, though I am not made
So find respite within the shade
And dab the beads of sweat down foreheads run,
An Indian pun.

102.

I come with games, stay while they last,
Tie down your clocks I'll move them fast,
Have me make someone else's, point
It's all in jest don't get disjointed
Just for me, not cups nor boxes, drums;
In barrels come.

103.

It comes from me, I mean it comes
To stern though never cold or glum,
But to the back, across the ship,
Up up I go, the vessel dips
And crashes, beating on the waves, such ride;
I'm here to stop the tide.

104.

I legless stand and armless reach,
But moveless cannot further breach,
Don't think, but am, come to my grange
And watch me as my colours change
And tap my sweetheart rivers, eh,
That waffle on all day.

105.

You're here though not by your intent,
You came but wish you'd sooner went,
Your name is all that holds you back
Or silence where your name does lack
While everything is busy and it seems all disappear;
Inevitably, you're still here.

106.

Across the battered shores I topple; fall,
But here I stand a longer name to call
I mark a change, now frantically they bustle,
Fill your holes and through my blankets rustle,
Soon you'll sleep and in your homes you'll dine;
Your years of mine.

107.

I come in many different shapes and sort,
You use me just the same, to port;
To have or take me at the edge;
And anxiously you losses hedge,
But not sure, pressure's building, you're in what? You've lost the plot;
I'm hot.

108.

I slither 'cross the ground I shake,
I'm ravenous, such flesh intake
My prey is drawn in mystic hobble,
Many mouths and stomachs gobble
If your thoughts have gone and lost their me,
You're left empty.

109.

I'm quick, as fast as you can think,
So through your mind I am a blink,
A moment, blinding, then I'm far
And in the pan, a short-lived star;
Recall the embers burning, wrack, retrace my track;
I'm back.

110.

I'm coming so you best be ready,
Hide away, I churn a steady
Tumult, but I also bring
My wonderland, where angels sing,
And on the top a thin veiled thread that covers all as brides are wed,
But in the middle; I am dead.

111.

If lucky laugh, if not then cry,
But either way to me they fly
And piles of paper stacked up flat,
Me on something; you count on that
Buy one for two and give a tip as token;
For I'm broken.

112.

I'm easy as from duck to do,
Just cut my parts up, bring it to,
We're thick as peas but do me up;
And makes me stronger, for you sup
In thick or thin, in trouble slip,
It's me you're in.

113.

I'm full of fires, yet don't burn
The food I give you'll have to earn,
That's everything but in me sinks,
That's everything of which you'll think
So if it's hot don't scream or shout, don't pout;
You best get out.

114.

You know you've got a me, on it
You place your hand and twist a bit,
A little fragile me, with care
I help you move from here to there,
I help you go but now all's gone awry;
Jump from me, off you fly.

115.

Four walls, no window, not a door,
I'm used though fleetingly to store
What you don't eat or drink, but sit in,
Even if I'm full you fit in,
All's gone wrong, too late perhaps too early;
Take an early me.

116.

There's none like me so from me start,
I'm where you stay and leave your heart,
And with the cows at dusk, come back
And at me, make yourself a snack
You cut, you mix and knead, you know what's in it as the butter's weighed;
I'm made.

117.

An ocean bed I hold the seas
In summer's heats that tumult, wheeze
My mouth profane takes lucky shots
In French, though not a French word taught,
You ought not look, I'm rather shy,
You'll stick me on standby.

118.

My head is full of holes, no pain,
My body made of one whole vein,
I celebrate your baby born,
Your wedding day with gifts adorn,
So mostly love me but the brisk
Winds howl about my risk.

119.

I stand or lean against the wall,
I'm high or low, not short or tall,
It's ready, fresh, it just came off,
Not perfect but too fair to scoff,
Too difficult decisions are, too tough to yet agree;
Put it on me.

120.

Let's talk me while the work is good
I'll chop, so first let's pop the hood
And in me all the goods are lined,
They set me up! I think you'll find
You're safe, don't worry, I'll not force or threat;
Don't sweat.

121.

All shapely liquors I anoint,
In fact each differs, that's my point;
If you hold me, all points assess,
I'm sure I'll lead you to success,
Less I'm on you with golden locks,
I shake my head, your passage blocks.

122.

A thousand types and more if mixed
All come from just a few first fixed
And nailed to a grand old mast,
I'll speak of origin and caste,
So cast not under false across the blue,
But show one's true.

123.

As waterfalls may topple down,
In those colliding waters drown,
Sometimes I roll up high, down fast,
Make little children cry, downcast,
Resigned to me, through life and, lo!
Along the seaside go.

124.

Tap my face and enter me;
There's space for all, choose one, two, three,
But shift along, here comes a queue
And this spells trouble, where are you?
My body's lined and ribbed with blocks;
You'll need a plank of locks.

125.

I'm long and short but both the same,
I measure space in two stock names;
One like what checks your hunger, though
The other makes sweet serum flow,
An starts the second, first an a,
I once was big, but small today.

126.

I've many mouths that open, close,
Aligned atop in totem rows
I eat all sorts, though never fat,
Drop me, I'm under, hidden that
I'm simple; store don't create, not the smartest;
Plethora of artists.

127.

It has my blood and lies on rocks,
A sentry like the sky and talks
Of dull and downcast things it weeps
A century, all misery heaps
Up death has come and to the screen;
The devil and my sea between.

The Mischievous Stripling

There once was a mischievous stripling,
Who'd hurl stones in the pond until crippling,
The fish in his way,
And made home for the day,
The water left restlessly rippling.

128.

Eat me though I'm light, not air,
So pump by choice your body tears,
And strike, you see I'm hot and bother do
With my fist see them follow you;
I'm strong, hold houses, trains I can,
As I'm a super man.

129.

I count to ten but oh, I'm slow,
In all, four times to ten I go,
I jest you not, lest I count short,
I need a full attentive court
The royal couple, knave or knight,
All sit with me till I count right.

130.

I am a grid within a ring,
No numbers, marks or anything,
But swing my tail, head'll move,
And make me as you do to prove
Your effort, no one doubts that from the sound;
Make fast what's round.

131.

It's just not right, not fair,
Get in a me and dance with ruffled hair
And feathers as a swan,
My last big work and then I'm gone,
Don't drill or dig, but break, or quickly first
Into me burst.

132.

I count your days, the end is near,
I'm crunched and see that's it I fear
That any me of things could come,
I'm up but no need to be glum,
As one, a public enemy;
But safety in a group of me.

133.

It's light, but is it light as I?
So light, a mass of me that flies
Together all the same we strain
But slow and dull if in your brain,
But in a hat, be proud of that! Stand tall, sleep well in bed;
I'm underhead.

134.

I'm black and white and red, or as it goes,
I come in columns, come in rows,
In part each tough so have your wit;
I'll press you judge, find weak from fit,
Though many, seems I'm often run
An angry one.

135.

I'm stronger than the court and king,
As legendary death I bring
Me, hold the line with all the same,
We'll rule the bridge and hold 'em, game
Is fixed, and I'm called what I'm called,
A tool, though never hauled.

136.

I'm all around you, never go,
Though to me you're as black as crow,
So forward see your face is lost,
Best left or right as nose embossed,
As if you wear an Eastern shawl
And hang me on the wall.

137.

You paid as if they'd captured me,
The most, which is quite fittingly
What I have, since I climbed to top
The tallest turret, hill or...stop!
You ape, it's not for you but mind don't hurl!
Gently! The girl!

138.

A sultan, king, khan or kalif,
The strong are longer, short are brief,
I'm firm but straight, command quite surely,
Measure increments, so purely
Draw the line just where I stand;
Three-hundred soldiers on my hand.

139.

Ten one's or otherwise one ten,
That's one in twelve, like other men,
Fact: half of me is silver-white
And with it I'm a common blight
Er, no, how inappropriate a gripe;
Should speak in stars and stripes.

140.

I'm black and white and tread all over
Little soldiers lead to rove, stir
To the beat as on parade,
But off and see their steps unmade,
When high the climax verberates a secret show?
Then low.

141.

Ruby, topaz, aquamarine,
Most valuable in me is seen,
I sit prestigiously on top,
Uneasy lies this noble prop
And when he fell and tumbled down, in water soaked;
I broke.

142.

I'm square, four corners, though three-de-
Tach two and pull my skin from me
An ornament, and cut my skin?
Take from another one a pin
And stitch me up again, I'm tattered though;
I'll take the blow.

143.

I'm friendly, I'm for love extended
Surely we'd half be best friended,
Did this street rat win the scruff?
I live in sands and in the rough,
I'm hard, cut me? You tickle, impish elf;
I'll cut myself.

144.

Intellects, news casters know
My English is most proper, so
I'll perk my lips and shake my wrist,
Won't drag, dress well, you get the gist;
Behave as well I should then rest the state - my head;
Where I've the biggest bed.

145.

I'm often bought, though no clear use,
I'm full, ate beads, foam, sheep or goose
And sit, I sit up off the floor,
So lean on me I'll help you, or
At penny-pinching partners throw,
For I will I the blow.

146.

I'm tall and strong, a keep and keep
A spinning wheel, all fall asleep
In clouds I'm built, though dreams unseen,
I own a king, speak not of queens,
Great posture stands a stone dry pose,
When all about me water flows.

147.

Ice bracelets hang from each staunch wrist,
As wax drips hot into each fist,
You bring the light, I hold the stuff,
Enough! To bed with but a puff
I'm up above though I hang low,
And in the chamber, beau.

148.

Avoid? No, into me you run
Declare what must be done be done
With waving flags begin the act;
Break both your legs, though less abstract,
Get out you sheep, you drone, you white faced clone;
This is my zone.

149.

A line of rounded bleached-white teeth,
No lips or gum then underneath
Just smooth white skin;
A young Boleyn.
A web-like pattern delicate that buffs
Around your scruff.

150.

No hole, yet in me you go down,
They came and saw, then went to town,
They took your king, check! Toppled queen,
They emptied out your parlour clean,
I'm bitter, from my jaws a batch
Of not me they did snatch.

151.

I'm not in jest, it's serious,
My money's gone mysterious
'We don't know how!' the adults say,
Though I know they do love to play
Me and the children tell the truth, no spoof;
This is my proof.

152.

You made your own, now it's too late
But really you'll not see me wait
Until you're gone, I'll tell you what,
Take it to me, a secret plot;
That I'm a plot you'll never learn;
So in me over turn.

153.

My heart that burns runs head to foot,
And leaves no single speck of soot
And held to someone high or low,
About the holder more I show
And when you're tired, life takes toll, I tend
To work both ends.

154.

Main entry is an answer; key,
A guff, remark, retort or plea,
I'm not how you then make suggestions,
Anti-what-you-call a question,
Actually a dinosaur of articles am I,
Oh, and reply.

155.

You have but one, though I change much;
I'm soft or sharp but can't be touched
Me my opinion at the top,
Together I am stronger, stop
And lower or you all can raise,
Me, throw me, what a haze.

156.

Come catch me, though it's not a hunt;
So cry a weapon, climb in front,
You're inside though said to be on,
From where you were you've upped and gone,
Prepare you fool, I might be quite bumpy;
You're taken for a me.

157.

Me me on as it might be rough,
I've held through worse, my clasp is tough,
I'm where you are when sat not still
Stop you go through the window, sill
A beam but softer, string but strong, I clad
This me-ing lad.

158.

Lift up your hand, fingers erect,
Your numbers did outnumber, checked
Now measured, something you had not,
Through toil is something you've now got
And though a pretty penny never paid, a sacrifice
Came at what price?

159.

Ten horses gallop up-down prancing,
Never move but ever dancing,
Ride, what lark! Though not the bird,
It's penguins dance the longest word
We sing and all is well, the family bring
A happy moving ring.

160.

One and two, now it's your part;
Stamp, one and two, within your heart,
Trop trample, but the horse is dead,
The birds are in the bush instead!
Grab sticks and guns and see them, hit! There's one and two, so quit!
Me it!

161.

A weaker pen or parker nib
I quest to places dark and glib,
Where danger lurks, smouldering breath
And pretty lips sleep half in death
Forget me not! Take back your words, breathe in each lung,
For I'm unsung.

162.

I'm given up? Find the last me
And filled, know anything might be,
The Ant, who took me high into the sky,
Your heart is cross, concludes I die.
I must be good, be bound to heaven, well
I'm not in hell.

163.

I'm played though not all players know
Inside and most are clueless, though
Aside sometimes beneath me there's
A poignant mark on real affairs
And though I'm never cleaned, please don't get shirty,
Only sometimes dirty.

From My Girlfriend's Collection

I lent my girlfriend some money. The next day she didn't pay it back. The day after she said she forgot. So the day after that I stuck a carrot in a fork and hung it from her room ceiling. I led a female deer into her room, who naturally stood under the carrot trying to reach it. When my girlfriend came in, she screamed, and I shouted, 'fork over the doe!'

164.

Proportions odd,
A long I plod
And me around,
From flowers drowned,
From fear you go;
I am cool, row!

165.

I speak, you nod though don't agree,
Agreeable to your ears me,
My memory it stays in stead
It runs around inside your head,
But now's the time to stand your place, so moment brace
And to me face.

166.

I am the same to the whole sum,
The loaf of bread or just a crumb,
Waves lash on pebbles where I fit,
I'm fine, not sterling I'll admit
I'm wrote and read quite different fashions,
Note, most want to lose my rations.

167.

I'm over you so watch my steps,
Pray on on me, I'll raise your rep
Utation, though if I'm raised, dipped,
And beat the nothing, find me clipped
And though you're not prepared, don't up and quit;
Me it.

168.

I'm of good health, I sure am pretty,
Stand for you, lie land or city,
Strokes describe what happened true
As I'm a tad more perfect you
My value fills 'bout quarter a short story, frig
I'm big!

169.

No feathers and I'm not a bird,
With eyes that make your lemons curd
The furnace burns, the coals are lit
And fire spews from out the pit
Oh fools that chase me, empty men,
I'm waiting in my den.

170.

Don't look and rule, I'm open, upright,
Outsides hard and insides soft light;
Inkling? Left downright bemused?
Look up to me for that I am used
For all the tricks in me, some underhanded stealth;
Play by myself.

171.

You get me not by choice, and shout,
Though first you thought no one about,
You get the same, though try assuage
With each step through the set, each stage
Don't burn your house to me
The mouse let be.

172.

A cloud I move lucid and free,
From duck's off south I'm off and see
I lost my fish and hence distress
Though that's more for the Fish I guess,
This is my world, the Mariner's as well,
For here I come, if not comes hell.

173.

I've five long legs, though one's cut short,
And flails as I then cavort;
While chasing down the sun I blot
And eating, then I'm mostly hot,
I'm sleeping here, so let me lay,
For I will have my day.

174.

You use me once or twice a day,
Though cut my friends, mine's nicer way
I hold the things you can't much count,
I someone over, awe's amount
And life would be a better me,
If just full of cherry.

175.

It's rather hard to pin me down,
Be me'd away and don a gown
When happy, in me high and good,
I build up as cold seasons should,
And you and I, we're much the same, we're kin, we're meant to be;
That's me!

176.

A foreign chicken missed the vet,
Collect from all the crowd a bet,
Now with a stick, don't swing but hit
And see your colours down a pit,
One box in which you all contain, no train
But special lane.

177.

I'm wise and so they beat me, oh
'It's your own fault', they said 'you know',
They're me but tough, I take the fall,
We're half the same but all in all
I'm nice, but watch them pass, I'm not so fast
So come in last.

178.

I'm big and rake the land, so dig straight moats,
I'll long the side and pull the boats,
Go to the water, take a drink, or nigh
I'll not, get off, I'm high!
Mysterious, I'm playful, trusting, strong and fierce, to battle or to frolic, lark;
I'm dark.

'Truly ruly red rubies rule luringly coolly.'

'How unfitting a recitation!'
'It fit perfectly into my mouth.'
'Well it must have been tasteless!
That, or unseemingly difficult to say.'

179.

If you see me I'm in your eye,
Can't get me out, you judge me, why
Not cut and dig, I'm not so deep,
Though I'll come back when you're asleep
I dance with clocks and candle sticks and feast;
And with the beast.

180.

Quiet! As if in a church,
Tucked-tail and left you in the lurch,
I lay my plans, they're half the best
Men take the mick, though meant in jest,
I most explore on days all done,
To holes skedaddle run.

181.

You're caught by me, though never chased,
I took you but 'twas I that braced,
'Twas I that snuck and whispered near
Till all a sudden I made clear,
And once I'm done, with smile or frown,
I'll never hide back down.

The African Lynx

I once saw an African lynx,
Caught under a cockatoo jinx.
Every fig that he found,
He'd stamp on the ground,
And then, with a smile, give two winks.

182.

I might be none, or two or three,
Or not, my name casts absentee
Quote me a cyclops may have caught;
Me here, or not alone distraught
I know, I need to know; your secrets safe, don't moan,
Just go away, I'm home.

183.

My branches thick with cushioned tips
And thorns project and through each rips
My top, the sun in muffled rays,
Dare sheer my beard right where I laze?
You take a slice but let's be fair,
All the remaining is my share.

184.

My shape; a female body full,
To take me one must downward pull,
My smell a sweet me-drop to lick
All's gone me shaped, so here's the trick:
Alone I face the air, though sister here and there,
Yet I'm a pair.

It's Pie

Ward baker head, three pies appoint,
One cream, for all, but one's anoint
With oil or pay five-and-nine, then
To go, he seeks it bless'd, amen.
Five-fingers mould the dough to tea
The fork cracks crust and sets all free
So clap our hands and give fives-high
As nigh no other's best it's pie.

185.

I'm long and slender, straight or bent,
The birds and beasts I most torment,
I give out fruit, or lead you there,
I make you shamed to be so bare
And if you can't see when we pass,
I'm in the grass.

186.

I me that you will rush as fools
To where's untrod by Angel mules,
But never me, I'm owned by God,
So put me in the quaking squad,
So put me under beds and in your heads and keep, don't peep;
I'll take your sleep

187.

I'm where the greatest two do meet,
No fish with fins nor beasts with feet,
Before it all, these two did clash,
The first against the second crash,
Yet one without the other drops, up prop secure,
I'm sure.

188.

Add me to all and much improved,
Though not to nicks or find you're moved,
Become a natural grounded me,
Though waters filled quite contrary
And don't believe it all, you're right to flinch,
Just take a pinch.

189.

In bag take me to market, sold
Expensive metal, home and bowled,
Not cold, I'm feeling! Miss the haul
As I remain in the same school
Find plenty creatures in the sea,
But not so many me.

190.

On cotton clouds the oceans swim,
I'm full of sense, I fill to brim,
My base is constant, holds the rest,
My top's diverse, differently dressed
Sometimes I fly by, quickly pick
And lift me up with sticks.

191.

The hardest part is now outside
And in the rest of it does hide,
Let's bring it out, it's shy and coy
But briefly, see the nut's like Troy's
First horse that banged, not rocked explosions knocked;
I'm shocked.

192.

I'm beautiful, though lost the plot
I'm over it, a clatter pot
Of pictures, words, of stories, names
All kept together in one frame.
A space for everything no cost,
But change so much I'm lost.

193.

When green you stop, when yellow go,
If red, too late, you missed the show,
I'm fruitful, breed when in the wild,
Captured, only man-made child,
Family is thought of wrong,
Hohum; I'm rounded long.

194.

I've two clear tails; one back one front,
So lined like colonel hath-I grunt,
No soldier I, but taught a king,
Babar rarar I toot and sing,
And don't forget I've two types be,
Remember that like me.

195.

In knives and spoons, mechanic faces,
Melted sand, in many places
Like you, permed, pressed, messy hair
I'm with you only if you're there,
You think like me on many things,
To flect again I fling.

196.

I walk the land and fly the air,
I swim the sea, touch me beware!
But kiss and all your dreams come true,
I'm in your throat, you're turning blue,
I sing a well-known throbbing pace,
I'm big for this small place.

197.

Though I've no legs, you'll find I walk,
Take me from someone else, they'll gawk,
They scold, you'll get a lot of me,
Despite the fact you find me free
And no one ever carries me in twos,
It's one they use.

198.

Express me well and manage it,
Or else your pot'll boil and spit
Not popular, though all the rage,
Beware you don't end in my cage
I sizzle, make you change into a thistle,
With me bristle.

199.

I'm near so jump and look around,
I'm at you, madly doing found
You run and climb the wrong damn tree
To find it covered too with me,
Go take a break and grab a bite as, curse,
You'll find me something worse.

200.

I start quite small like insect, march
And grow first clenched and back straight starched
I see it coming here it floats,
A ripple of discordant notes;
I pat it on its head, use tact;
Prevent it in me act.

201.

This book has all of me but one,
It vainly thinks to prayers it's come
To this; now check from front to back,
Me back? Don't quibble, sulk or slack,
But if you check so stupidly,
You'll get a stupid me.

Answers

'Two steps forward, one step back', said the hapless Frog from the well. 1) an bsujdiplf. 2) a xiffm. 3) a xiffm. 4) a rvftujpo. 5) a xijtqfs. 6) qbqfs. 7) a sjeemf. 8) a tlvmm. 9) a ipssps. 10) a ufbs. 11) a gbdf. 12) a ibu. 13) a qbqfsdmjq. 14) a cfmm. 15) a dijo. 16) an fbs. 17) a tpdlfu. 18) a xjoepx. 19) a csvti. 20) a njssps. **He heard it, then unheard it the other way.** 21) izjq. 22) a ctuspm. 23) xnpk. 24) a dtge. 25) a lmps. 26) a gqblf. 27) a dnna. 28) a qnoxuzjk. 29) a unofvd. 30) a hhgs. 31) a gqjdoctgjo. 32) dnuspm. 33) qzost. 34) a izoffq. 35) a lhtr. 36) a dgfdl. 37) thmj. 38) a unpsi. 39) a ahq. 40) a zzxm. **'Good job old boy. Hurrah! Hurray! Callay!'** 41) a iuhfnoh. 42) a ulqj. 43) fdvk. 44) a ilqjhu. 45) vwhho. 46) a joryh. 47) a kdqgvkdnh. 48) juhdvh. 49) vqrz. 50) a sdw. 51) a ehoob exwwrq. 52) a (fkdlu) dup. 53) a ods. 54) a exw. 55) wlq. 56) a exfnhw. 57) a krs. 58) a irrw. 59) a fdushw. 60) a vods. **Planned and made attempt but failed, back to the beginning hailed.** 61) a rgnd. 62) dmntfg. 63) a adks. 64) lnqd. 65) a aqthrd. 66) a knf. 67) bknfr. 68) a vntmc. 69) an zonknfx. 70) a vnmcdq. 71) a gtf. 72) a cqdzl. 73) mnqsg. 74) a lhqzbkd. 75) the gnqhynm. 76) dzrs. 77) rkzbj. 78) an dcfd. 79) rntsg. 80) a sqho.

From the Riddle Me Collection

A cat, a dog, a horse, a frog, no beast of air or water can a bear assuaged but not when raged, young child, not an adult man. 81) a klivomr. 82) irkperh. 83) the asvph. 84) aiwx. 85) a hec. 86) a firh. 87) ciwxivhec. 88) asvo. 89) a tewwtsvx. 90) a firgl. 91) a riawtetiv. 92) xshec. 93) xsqsvvsa. 94) eki. 95) a tixep. 96) lepj. 97) a ciev. 98) a womt. 99) a fyh. 100) wtvmrk. **I've an ace and a jack up my sleeve.** 101) twnoft. 102) gwo. 103) a tvfo. 104) a ncqnf vsgf. 105) a xcjvjphtpqn. 106) bwuwnp. 107) a tgbv. 108) a utbko. 109) a gnbui. 110) xkovft. 111) a ccom. 112) tqvr. 113) a lkueigo. 114) a icofmg. 115) a ccuj. 116) a iqng. 117) a qqu. 118) a tjpyft. 119) a tjfng. 120) a tjpr. **'What, are you hot?' asked the caterpillar, blowing a ring of smoke in her face, 'to get my questions make you sweat?'** 121) a nhb. 122) a frorxu. 123) a frdvwhu. 124) a nhberdug. 125) a phjdebwh. 126) a vhw ri gudzhuv. 127) (the frorxu) eoxh. 128) an lurq a sdfn ri sodblqj fdugv. 130) a (whqqlv) udfnhw. 131) a vrqj. 132) a qxpehu. 133) a ihdwkhu. 134) a furvvzrug. 135) the dfh ri vsdgh. 136) a vlokrxhwwh. 137) a nlqj. 138) a uxohu. 139) a glph. 140) a (sldqr) nhb. **Exhausted, she sat down for a brief respite. 'Give them back!' demanded the Opossum. 'All of them!'** 141) a xmjri. 142) a xpncdji. 143) a ydvhjiy. 144) a lpzzi. 145) a xpncdji. 146) a xvnogz. 147) a xcviyzgdzm. 148) a rvm. 149) a (kzvmg) izxfgvxz. 150) a yzazvo. 151) a ajjg. 152) a bmvqz. 153) a xviygz. 154) a ocznvpmpn. 155) a qjdxz. 156) a mdyz. 157) a nomvk. 158) a qdxojmt. 159) a hzmmt-bj-mjpiy. 160) a wzvo. **I'm in haphazard disarray, I'll bet on cinque and sice today.** 161) a nlxv. 162) nvvl. 163) a pvql. 164) a isudt. 165) sbypi. 166) a vvauj. 167) a cptn. 168) a vpiaayk. 169) a jygnuu. 170) a hvur. 171) a lyonna. 172) chzlx. 173) a jvm. 174) a hvcs. 175) ywoyoa. 176) a vvus. 177) a mbe. 178) a nvxzk. 179) hlgbzf. 180) a svazk. **'Each single, also all alike', said the Meerkat to the next. 'How inconsistent!'** 181) twutwozm. 182) oq rrj. 183) a mkrr. 184) a qgdv. 185) a tpdoj. 186) ggdv. 187) a tjrvj. 188) tcox. 189) a hqohkozp. 190) a qkhgj um adcsu. 191) a tjhpq. 192) a nkqh. 193) a ccqesg. 194) an fnhtmgub. 195) a sgipjiaqxx. 196) a gtrk. 197) a tvlgp. 198) bpjiw. 199) a ccuo. 200) bpwmhowicszz.

Explanations

If you've addressed each problem with its proper title and unfolded each solution into the stories it only hid, allow me here to explain what remains. To explain as palms do from fists, as blossoms do from buds, and as the drowsy Butterfly did from its homely chrysalis.

I shan't pick up every hint dropped, but only the obscurer ones, along with comments and backdrops to some of the scenes set. My endeavour has only been much like an allergy, causing me to do no more than scratch the surface, and has resulted in scenes far more like most healthy foods, needing to be taken with a pinch of salt. Though I'm aware of the fulsomeness of the English language in its dialects, most of these scenes ascribe to British English, and British cultural references.

1.

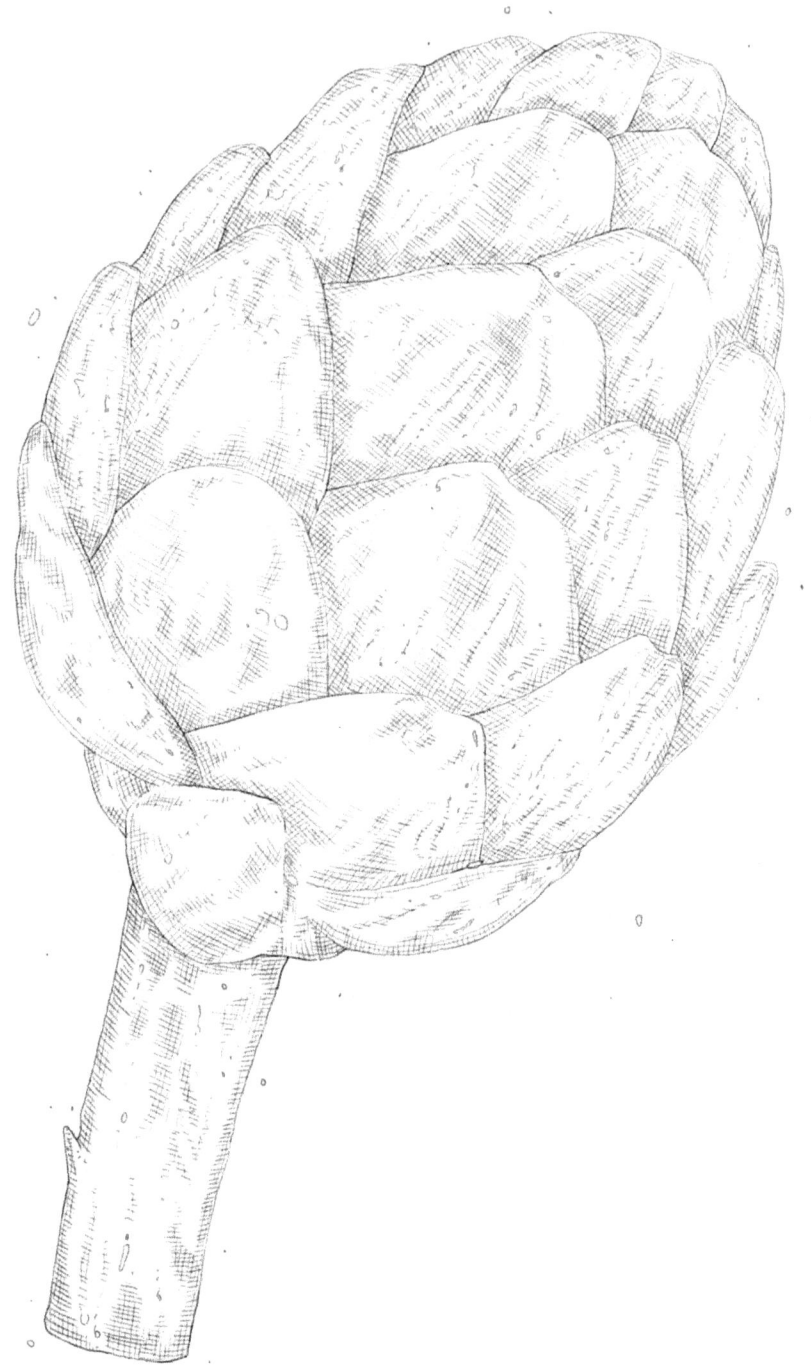

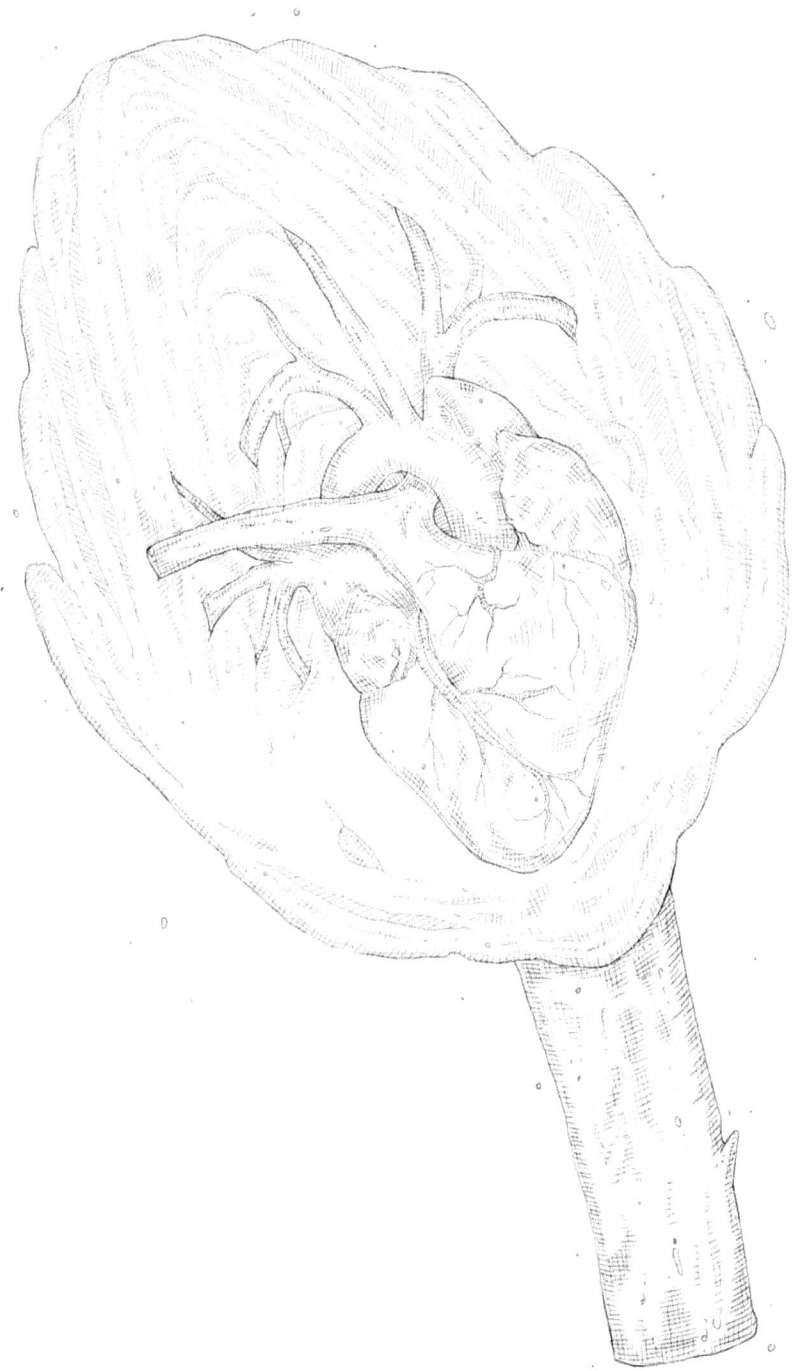

2.
I spin, and round and round not dizzy, like a spinning top and busy turning - the wheels are turning, an idiom meaning a process has started and something is happening.
be at me resigned to never first, always behind - be at or behind the wheel.
but careful, dreams will bring your death they weep; at me don't fall asleep - to not fall asleep at the wheel.

3.
I have no mouth but there a spoke put in me, on such words I choke - to put a spoke in the wheel.
see fortune's me, luck's where it lands - wheel of fortune, known as the title of a TV game show, took its name from the Babylonian, ancient Greek, and then Medieval philosophical concept of *Rota Fortunae*, the changeable nature of Fate. The wheel, spun by the goddess Fortune, would change all positions on it, for better or worse.
but where a two and one more nuisance spurred; a third - a third wheel.

4.
I pose though no one takes a picture - to pose a question.
lead to science or to scripture - a question of science, or a question of religion.
both are out of me it seems - to be out of the question.
I'm smart, there's nothing else I'd be - there's no such thing as a stupid question.
move on, just love; pop me - to pop the question, to appear or put suddenly, is recorded from 1725 in the citation 'Dear Governor and Governess, the boy here having given me leave to ask you how you do, I have made bold to pop the question to you'. The expression became synonymous with a proposal of marriage from the 19th Century.

5.
I'm quiet as a mouse backstage, till curtains up and play-writes rage - a stage whisper has to be loud as is intended to be heard by the audience, but gives the impression that it is inaudible to others on stage.
but change when on east porcelain - east porcelain, or china, which took its name from the country. Chinese whispers, known as *telephone* in the United States, is a game where a message is whispered between players until it is undoubtedly altered in a humorous way. The connotation that Chinese is confusing and incomprehensible dates back to Europeans in the 1600s, though can be seen as offensive in modern culture, so perhaps should be changed to *crockery whispers*, though that seems quite difficult to say.

6.
I'm slender, one princess no pea - the 1835 Hans Christian Andersen fairy tale speaks of a young woman whose royal blood is tested with a pea. But were there no pea, it would leave only a smooth flat surface, as a sheet of paper.
and pure, how things look good on me - to look good on paper.
you seek me? Fine, I'll leave a trail - to leave a paper trail.
put cage to me; tell my tale - to put pen to paper.

7.
a raven and a desk to write - in Lewis Carroll's Alice's Adventures in Wonderland, the famous riddle is posed, 'Why is a raven like a writing-desk?'.
a language only talked in tongues - to talk in riddles or tongues.
in squirming insects covered, bung - to be riddled or infested with something.
I'm what I am - I'm a riddle.

8.
it shan't get through; my walls are thick - to get something through someone's thick skull.

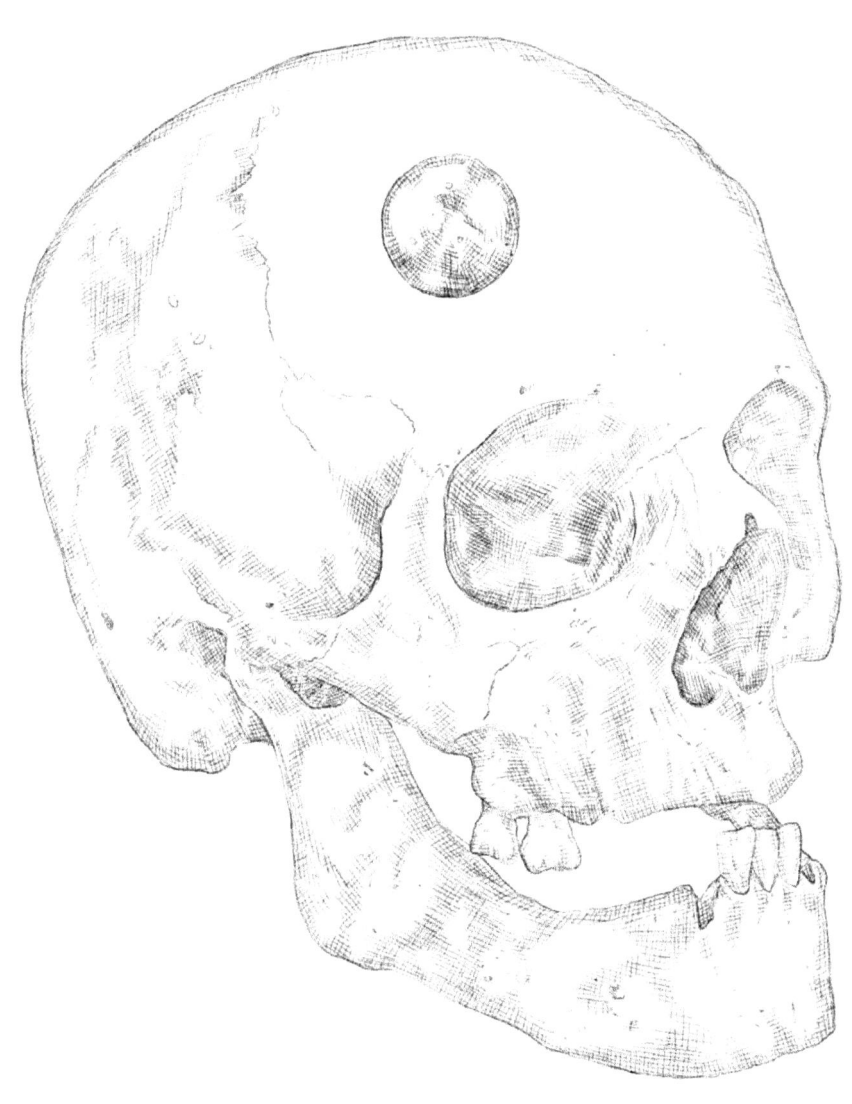

9.
in me you throw your hands up - to throw one's hands up in horror.
behave or it's straight to bed and still hungry; you little me - to be a little horror, or unruly child.

10.
wine, salt and I, we bare your toil - blood, sweat and tears.
look the same as shreds left hung - tear as in to cry, and tear as in what is done to paper, are homographs.
but sound to some as layers strung - to tear as in to cry, and tier as in layered, are homophones in many English accents.
in barrage, comes your core with ease - to cry one's heart out.
and bursts you into mes - to burst into tears.

11.
I can't be short, but can be long - to have a long face.
I'm it! Accept and head out strong - face it! Also *head out* is a more direct reference to the outward side of your head.
you can't buy me but value check - face value.
I'm never full but stuffed, bedecked - to stuff one's face.
bedecked with one tall mountain, upwards stretching crane; it's just as plain - to be as plain as the nose on one's face.

12.
I'm made by someone madly raving - the Mad Hatter, though never directly referred to as such in the book, is a character from Lewis Carroll's Alice's Adventures in Wonderland.
from me I'll pull on someone's ears - to pull a rabbit out of a hat.
so off I come, the job well done, surprising feat - to take one's hat off to someone.
surprising feat; myself I'll eat! - to eat one's hat.

13.

14.
at the ball, just mee, let's dance - the belle of the ball.
hear me and all the whistles prance - with bells and whistles, or with extra fancy adages.
there aft you want to go again? Give them a me and just say when - to give someone a bell, or a call.
not sour, sweet, no taste but heavens; oranges and lemons - oranges and lemons is a traditional English nursery rhyme that lists the bells of the churches of the City of London. Sung by children while playing an old game where pairs make arches whilst the rest run through. In the last line the children in the middle are caught, much like an early version of musical chairs.

15.
I'm up, so keep me there old chap - to keep your chin up.
so use me, wag me, now with chums - to wag one's chin, or have a good chinwag, is an expression meaning to chat or gossip.
and take it on me, what e'er comes - to take it on the chin.
just drink it up like cups of tea, let's laugh and be merry, me me - chin chin, an expression of salutation, often used for gratitude or congratulations, though out of use now, even in the green pastures of England.

16.
give me to me, I'm everywhere - to give ear to someone and listen closely.
I'm everywhere, in corn and wheat - an ear of corn.
the trees, take care! - the trees have ears.
in pigs, though that's a mess I fear - to make a pig's ear of something.
a snow-topped range from me to me, though only when happy - to grin from ear to ear, showing all of one's white teeth.

17.
so eyes fix straight to me and stay - an eye socket.
but note, I take no shoe, just cotton seems I like to hit, how rotten! - to sock it, or hit something hard and far.
mind, don't prod me, push or barge; I'm positive, I'll charge - an electrical socket. Electrical sockets charge electrical devices, while positive alludes to the electrical polarity of positive and negative.

18.
and let me crack my mouth comes heavy breaths from north and south - to crack the window open.
I'm bought, though spend none, take none home, not free - to go window-shopping.
but opportunity - a window of opportunity.

19.
you're just as daft - to be as daft as a brush.

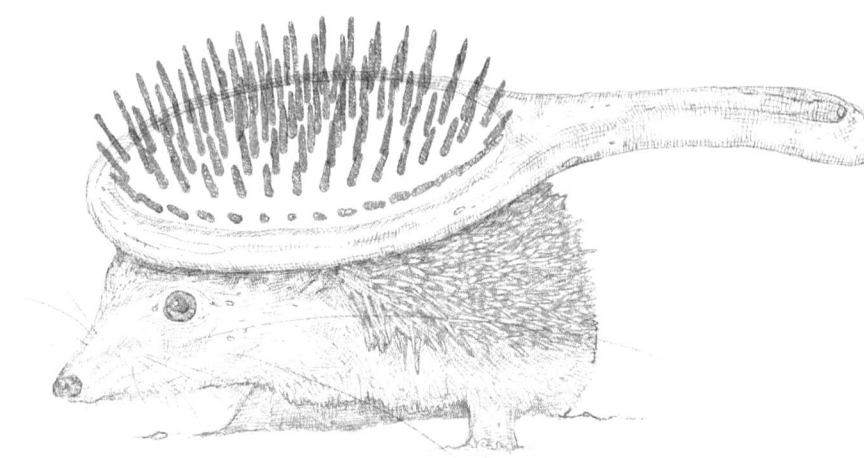

20.
I am a trick, I'm all but smoke - to be all smoke and mirrors.
I see where snow has settled merrily, I'm on the wall; so call - the German folk tale 'Snow White' told of the Evil Queen, who would repeat, 'Magic mirror in my hand, who is the fairest in the land?' The story later adapted by Disney moved the mirror from hand to wall, though other possible influences include the hung mirror of Maria Sophia Margaretha Catherina von Erthal's evil step-mother.

21.
and out of place I angry rave - to have or put a hair out of place.
don't startle me, I'll raise and in the moment - to be hair-raising, or scary.
in the moment, cross, confound chagrin - to be in the cross hairs.
so cut me, crush me, burn; where e'er I sit, I don't know what to do, I'm split - to have split-hairs.

22.
I'm pushed and down - to push a button.
but when I'm lined, at last not done - the final suit or waistcoat button should never be done up. There are a few theories behind this peculiar etiquette ranging from ease to ride horseback to the fashion of young dandies to wear two layers of waistcoats so needing to show the second off. However, I prefer the theory that says that Edward VII put on some weight, so much so that he couldn't do up the final button of this waistcoat, and so as not to embarrass the king, the entire court followed suit.
so hit me right and make it true - to hit the button, much like to hit the nail on the head.
I'll make a brighter you - to be as bright as a button.

23.
a cloud, I gaily float around, until I fall sheer to the ground - sheer and shear are homophones.
and die, in me you're strongly fixed, won't change so pull me up betwixt - die and dye are homophones. To be dyed-in-the-wool means to be of strong, fixed opinion.
so pull me up betwixt your eyes, the world, you've had enough - to pull the wool over someone's eyes.

24.
and off-me, do without a thought - to do something off-the-cuff, or spontaneous.
if I won't close, no hex or jinx, you need a couple links - to use cufflinks.

25.
I'm half, not underhand, I slip - all are types of knot; a half knot, an overhand knot, and a slipknot.
go figure, hate that Great old sword that challenge cut of its accord - as legend would have it an intricate knot of cornel bark

bound an ox-cart to a post in the land of Gordium. When Alexander the Great arrived, he took it upon himself to untie the knot, but it being impossible to untie, he thought outside the box and cut it open with one swing of his sword, thus solving the impossible problem. Perhaps it doesn't bode well for the great minds of the time that none thought of cutting the knot, but Zeus was so happy he sent a thunderstorm as an omen that Alexander the Great would become king of all Asia.
but take two lovers, husband bride, with which a cord is tied - to tie the knot, or to wed.

26.
I word it special ways, and then - to frame something, or express something, in particular words.
because of me you're caught and penned - to frame someone or set someone up.
you think what's in me's good or bad? Then find a me of mind - one's frame of mind.

27.
I'm run and through it all you'll find the things you'd by chance left behind - to run a comb through something.
light, though through that beach it clatters - to comb the beach looking for something.
silent brushed each dental edge, hedge sheath; how fine my teeth - to go over something with a fine-tooth comb.

28.
from greater beasts, when one I plumb, when two from different critters come - a ponytail has one single bunch fastened at the back, but pigtails have a pair, worn either side of the head.
I'm chic and in or stale and out - fashions are so precarious.

29.
I'm with a cheek quite farcical - to be tongue and cheek.
and forcibly an arsenal - an arsenal of words.
I writhe and squirm and from me come, but nothing from those dumb - to be mute, unable or unwilling to speak. Old Saxon, Gothic and Old Norse all show roots of the term dumb to imply speechless. The term meaning foolish comes from Old High German influences in Middle English.

30.
from far places, Greek beware! - beware of Greeks baring gifts, and ancient proverb no doubt inspired by the Trojan War and the inaptly named Trojan (Greek) Horse.
string gab together, weave a spell for with me given you speak well - to have the gift of the gab.
with hands and heart make art of me - a hand-made gift.
redundantly I'm free - a free gift is a pleonasm, the use of more word parts than are necessary. Examples include, under false pretences, a frozen tundra, to veer off course, a safe haven, and our redundant expression here, a free gift.

31.
first you meet to make a bloody big boat only for you, buddy - a friend ship.
sometimes more green when hedges hide - a hedge between keeps friendship green, a proverb on the benefits of some level of privacy.
an end that drifts apart but starts up cruelly; you strike me - to strike up a friendship.

32.
the tips of cues made from my buds - Q-tip, a generic trademark in American English for a cotton bud.
picked in the farms, the righteous floods - God sent floods in response to how great the wickedness of the human race has

become, Genesis 6:5, while the early cotton industry in the United States relied on the slave trade for labour.
on, see it's time to get me on - cotton on to something, to grasp the reality of something.
so bless that child, bless her soul that shines; her socks of mine - bless her cotton socks.

33.
punch, I was a boxer briefly - boxer shorts, or briefs.
fancy me, a smarty chiefly - to be a fancy-pants, or a smarty-pants.
running 'round all hither-thither - to pant or be panting from running around.
ants fill me and stop your dither - to have ants in your pants.
dally, folly frolic all 'round town; you're caught me down - to be caught with your pants down.

34.
I like the powerful and rich, on them I'm me, get some for which - to be a hanger on, someone who follows the rich and powerful in hopes to get some advantage or financial gain from the relationship.

35.
and blow, I float, I'm clearly caught, I know - to blow a kiss.
I happen but I'll tell you not - to not kiss and tell.
I'll bring you life and breath, last shot - the kiss of life.
last chance to see, farewell and me, don't cry; for I'm goodbye - to kiss something goodbye.

36.
I'm dizzy, all I do is turn - to turn the other cheek.
you lose an eye and then you learn - an eye for an eye, as opposed to the expression to turn the other cheek. Ironically both teachings are derived from Biblical writings.
to decorate me roses red - to have rosy cheeks.
then put them in another's bed - to put the roses in someone's cheeks. Bed refers to a flower bed.
but that's some me right there, risky you sprung - some cheek.
risky you sprung, I ate your tongue - tongue-in-cheek.

37.
and smooth, it softly falls on skin - to be as smooth as silk.
but find a sow's ear cursed, adverse to make my purse - you can't make a silk purse out of a sow's ear, a proverb from the common perception of swine as unrefined.

38.
and four a kind I quickly grew at first I cut, and then I bark, the third and forth both bury. Hark! - the first teeth from the front are incisors, then canines, and finally first and second molars.

39.
I me along, both smooth and fast - to zip along.
I past someone, they see me by - though grammar implies an error, as it should read 'I passed someone', *I* is in fact the verb, and it is a reference to the expression to zip past someone.
In fact, as I go up I fly! - a fly in one's trousers is closed by the zip, often used synonymously.
you moan, when you're with me you're still I move, you move I sit; me it! - zip it! Or to tell someone to stop talking.

40.

41.
I find what's open, not what's closed - freckles develop on exposed skin, not covered skin. Freckles form due to exposure to UV-B radiation increasing the cell production of melanin, triggered by sunlight.

42.
my voice I threw - to ring, a direct reference to the sound such as a telephone rings.
I'm on your ear - an earring.
and in it too - a ringing in the ears.
less planets, Mercury, the Sun, Venus, Earth, Mars; show-off and run - this hint is two-fold. The planets listed here are the planets that do not have planetary rings, hence 'less', while the list of planets orbit, or 'run' rings around the sun.
and when you're sure your love's not spent, present - an engagement ring.
I'm busy sent - an engagement ring is also an indication of being busy or occupied, such as on the telephone.

43.
I'm cold and hard, it's easy that way - cold hard cash.
that way, give me credit - cash or credit.
I'll talk, chat, say - money talks.
problems flowing - a cash flow problem.
I won't be made? It takes time - to make some cash.
I am heavy weighed all the options? Placed a bet? Came tops? Chinchin! You win! I'm in - to cash in on something or to cash something in.

44.
a row of numbers, doubles made - fingers or digits.
though one foul pair doth masquerade - the thumbs.
I'm green, though not from envy dabble - to have green fingers.
rest, don't lift me feet up, babble on - to not lift a finger.
for if you work too hard; ungrown, you'll leave me bone - to work one's fingers to the bone.

45.
iron me, but full of air - steel is an alloy of iron and other elements such as carbon.
I'm stronger with each bond, I share - the inclusion of the other elements such as carbon to iron increase the tensile strength and act as hardening agents.
my nerves, you take them, keep them close - to have nerves of steel.
show them and show my strength the most - to show one's steel, or to show one's metal, to display bravery.
the most against, so me your heart and see you can - to steel one's heart against something, strengthen your resolve.
as I own superman - the man of steel. *The Man of Steel* is the 1986 mini-series on the origins of Superman and the subscript name of the American comic book series that ran from 1991 to 2003. Additionally in 2013 the British-American film featuring the DC Comics character Superman was given the same name.

46.
I'm fit, compare all else to me - to fit like a glove.
takes time to wear me, out foxy - fox gloves. Foxgloves are a flower, whose namesake seems to still be under etymological debate. It has been propose to originally, in fact, refer to folk's gloves, folk's being the kind of fairies in Shakespeare's Midsummer Night's Dream, 'In Welsh this flower is called by the beautiful name of *maneg ellyllon*, or the fairies' glove.

Now, in the days of our ancestors, as everyone knows, these little elves were called in English 'the good folks' (Talbot, 1847). But, as every one knows, Anatoly Liberman writes in his Oxford University Press blog, that 'belief in fairies, as in *Midsummer Night's Dream*, has no roots in Old English, so all talk about good folk's glove(s) lacks foundation'. Well, there we go then.
get out! A spider-less three legs - a glove has only five 'legs', three less than a spider.
you think you're tough? You think I won't stand on my own? I'm soft? I'm off! - the gloves are off.

47.
my gold is dubious but settled good and bad; a nettled petal - a golden handshake.

48.
work harder, dip your elbow in - to have or give it some elbow grease.
and put it on their palms, a sin that makes it all go faster, right! - to grease someone's palms.
that makes it all go faster, right! That's why the thunder lost to light - greased lightening. The observation that greased machinery runs faster, as fast perhaps as black-leather clad lightening, as in the 1978 classic movie Grease. However it is not because a lightening flash is greased that it is faster than a thunderclap, but because the speed of light is faster than the speed of sound in air.
though some by hand may place it, shape it, there - referring to hair products such as gels and wax. Petroleum based pomades actually containing real grease and fatty ingredients to give it that shine and hold.
best wash your hair - to have greasy hair.

49.
my man, you'll catch your death of heat, so here's a carrot not to eat - a snowman.
grab cotton pads and caste them out - snowballs.
you're under me? Abundant drought! - to be snowed under.
no school or work, a call to play, away! For it's my day - a snow day.

50.
a means to bake a cake; just sing - Pat-a-cake, pat-a-cake, baker's man is 'one of the oldest and most widely known surviving English nursery rhymes' according to its Wikipedia page. Sung in accompaniment with a clapping game by children, it appears in Mother Goose's Melody, 1765.
a way, still down, to make it flat - to pat something down.
a postman with a two-toned cat - Postman Pat, a British stop-motion animation television series about a local postman called Pat, and his black and white cat, first screened in 1981.
a manner calms or says well done and thwack, on head - to pat a dog on the head.
and back - a pat on the back.

51.
another name a great sea boat - navel and naval are homophones.

52.
lean on me when you're not strong, I'll be there if where I belong - though not a clue, the first true lines are a homage to Bill Withers for the song Lean on Me, ranked one of the greatest songs of all time.

53.
in me chance dropped a strange affair - to drop something in someone's lap.
now me it up and make the most - to lap something up.
in luxury of mine you boast - to be in the lap of luxury.
well done old boy! Superb! Kudos! Your victory! Go take a me - to take a victory lap.

54.
no me, you hate to hear us all, or if, just do the job you bawl - no ifs or buts.
though wait however they all plea defy, one shan't comply all me - all but one.
I'm gone, farewell, adieu to you, I'm rotten; not forgotten - to be gone but not forgotten.

55.
hold in me what keeps - foods that keep can be stored in tins.
my errors scold and put me like a cat on top - a cat on a hot tin roof, describes being nervous.
where music beats but my ears bop - to have a tin ear, or to not understand or appreciate music.
Alors, mon dieu! The clue's a key; the case afoot, so send meme - Les Adventures de Tintin is a popular comic series about a young reporter come sleuth created by the Belgian cartoonist Georges Remi, otherwise know as Herge.

56.
I'm kicked not hurt, but now you're dead - to kick the bucket.
all left a hole my dearest Liza - There's a Hole in My Bucket is an old folk song sung between the characters Henry and Liza. The song probably originates from the German folk song Heinrich und Liese, which became popular as a commercium song, traditional academic songs sung at feasts as tablerounds.

now you're gone, though most the points you missed upon my list - a bucket list, things to achieve before dying.

57.
I'm mad? Well if so made by you! The Hare in Spring now sprung anew - to be hopping mad.
anew brew made from me - hop, used as a flavouring and stability agent in beer.
so me to it - to hop to it.
can't stop, I'm bound to change, too long the same I'm vexed; what channel's next? - channel hopping.

58.
'my me!' I said, you took offence - my foot! An informal expression for strong contradiction.
and sabotage, shot me in, whence - to shoot oneself in the foot.
was I alone put in the grave - to have one foot in the grave.
make sure that right not wrong, the first has gone - to put the right foot, your best foot, forward.
you get off on - to get off on the right foot.

59.
not open, best it's hid away, so under me and leave me lay - to sweep something under the carpet.
not you, for only kings unfurl for queens, lords, ladies, dukes and earls - to roll out the red carpet.
for street rats, magic, take a seat; see me move with no feet - Disney's Aladdin, the street rat, sat upon a magic flying carpet.

60.
my mark an insult, face head-first - a slap in the face, or anything as insulting.
but cant? To wrist or else far worse - a slap on the wrist.
I'm quick and dash, though carelessly, that's me - to be slap-dash, or careless.

61.
the first is dropped and then we wait, the other's coming though it's late - to wait for the other shoe to drop.
mind your edge - a pun; notice your advantage, and take care of the expensive leather.
though soft cow skin - leather.
you're one me in - to be a shoe in.

62.
you heard me, then you have me known - to have heard enough, and to know enough.
so leave, farewell, well me alone - to leave someone well enough alone.
speak to myself; can't 'thank you' me, decry - can't thank you enough.
decry that I is I - enough is enough.

63.
hush now, me up! And just admit - belt up! A strong expression to tell someone to be quiet.
'twas low a blow below me hit - to hit someone below the belt.
keep secrets, know your stuff, thoust wily thee; kept under me - to have something under one's belt.

64.
with me you couldn't have agreed - I couldn't agree more, an expression of strong support.
you bite me though you wish you'd not - to bite off more than you can chew.
despite, I make a merry lot - the more the merrier.
so plead sir, ask for me, but don't dare press - 'please sir, I want some more!' is the famous line of Oliver Twist in Charles Dickens' novel of the same name.
it's me or less - more or less.

65.
Look Mum

Look mum, me arms gone black an' blue.
'Cause Tom at school keeps hittin' me.
I tell 'im quit, me arms gone numb,
'e says it's all my fault, but mum,
It's like a black-'ole, see!

Well gosh, my love, it's not your fault.
This Tom's an awful creature.
Next time he hits you, raise your hand,
And quickly tell your teacher.

Furst it went green like what the sides of boats turn in salt wa'er,
Then it turned blue more like what clean jeans in the shops right ought'a.
But mum, 'e said cause I was talking all the time an' usin'
Language what 'e said was worse'n ears I was abusin'.
'e said me questions made no sense, I just asked what wa' aight 'n?
'e lost it 'n he grabbed me arm an' coloured good me skin.

My dear, come here and let me hug and kiss away the pain,
I'll bandage up your arm until you're feeling right as rain.
And next time this boy bullies you,
You tell your teacher quickly do,
It won't happen again.

But mum, I kicked 'im back and frew
Me books at 'im an' then me shoes,
'e packed his briefcase up an' quit
'e was a rubbish teacher, but
Least gave me this cool bruise.

66.
I make a pile burnt, so called - a log fire.
I make the box around, so walled - a log cabin.
I'm not the best though record keep, of data stacks and dates in heaps - a record of information, otherwise called a log.
I'm good with beats, and counting, sing; that I'm a rhythmic thing - log-a-rhythmic.

67.
no mind but what a clever me! - to be a clever clogs, a smart aleck, or generally someone too astute for their own good. The expression first appears as clever-boots, boots being synonymous with 'fellow' as far back as the early 1600s. Clogs being common footwear in England and around Europe, the phrase came both naturally and with perfect alliteration. Interestingly, Aleck is a shortening of Alexander, and the expression possibly derives from the 19th century con man and thief Aleck Hoag.
I'm up, you're still until I drop - to clog something up.

68.
the canvas ripped, it grows more round - a laceration swells.
and opened up, it might be old, retell a story not since told - to reopen old wounds.
get over quick, that's in a lick. You're prime? - to lick one's wounds.
you're prime? Just give it time - time heals all wounds.

69.
you're me a sore, a poor excuse - be a poor excuse or apology for something.
I'll never come, won't budge a foot, and never made - to make no apologies.
I'm sorry, but is not me - sorry is an apology. However, 'sorry, but…' is a poor one if one at that.

70.
I work; see my effects enthral - to work wonders.
enthralled, beguiled, seven were great tombs and gardens, lighthouse, spur - the Seven Wonders of the Ancient World include the Great Pyramid of Giza, which is a tomb, the Hanging Gardens of Babylon, and the Lighthouse of Alexandria.
spur me on, and one day you'll succeed you dunce, just hit it once - to be a one hit wonder.

71.
I've got four arms all fixed to bend - two from each of the huggers.
the strongest is not lion, horse, not bull, not theirs; no, it's the Bear's - a bear hug.

72.
in me you fly up to the sun - from Greek mythology, Icarus attempted to escape Crete using wings made of feathers and wax. Though warned of hubris by his father, he flew too close to the sun, which melted the wax and he fell to the sea. The myth has very similar versions in other mythologies, for example in Hindu mythology where Jatayu raced to the sun but got his wings burnt and so was grounded to become a guide to the God Rama.
and fall, keep falling, get up! Run! In me you're chased but never caught - despite all the advocates of dream interpretation, recurrent dreams such as falling and being chased have been suggested to be remnants of our evolutionary history. The most common cause of infant death in chimpanzees is falling from trees. Whether as a startle mechanism to wake the sleeper up, or simply as a constant concern, these fears haunt us still today.
but never will you ever really be, though pray and plea, quite in your me! - in your dreams.

73.
just look up then and follow me - to the north, Polaris, or the north star, is particularly useful in celestial navigation as it sits approximately aligned with the Earth's axis of rotation.
how could you? You're not bird nor bee - migratory birds such as swallows fly thousands of miles to change climates in altering seasons. It is not known exactly how they navigate, but it is believed that birds rely on reading the sun's position, and then stars at night. Whether they can somehow feel the Earth's magnetic field or not seems to still be up for debate.
you sail the sea with pins that pull - with a compass.
until you find the true me - to find true north.
illuminating with my lights - the Northern Lights, or Aurora Borealis. Named after the Roman goddess of dawn, Aurora.

74.
work me, perform and break the odds - to work miracles, perform miracles.
I'll feed with naught, make land of sea - across the Sea of Galilee, Jesus fed five thousand with just five small barley loaves and two small fish, the aptly named 'miracle of the five loaves and two fish'. Meanwhile, in the Book of Exodus, when fleeing the Egyptians, Moses divided the waters of the Red Sea so the Israelites could go through on dry ground.

75.
and soon on me you'll find your grander dreams are near to hand - on the horizon, imminent or becoming apparent.
one I'll expand - to expand one's horizon.

76.
I wake first as it's brighter here - the sun rises in the east.
my place is far or middle - the Far East, often now referred to as East Asia, and Middle East, formerly referred to as the Near East, are Eurocentric geographical terms.

between us we shall never meet - East is East and West is West and never the twain shall meet, the opening line of Rudyard Kipling's poem 'The Ballard of East and West' that has worked its way into becoming a common English proverb.
wherever then you go, know home's easy - East or West, home's best, another proverb indicating that no matter where you go, in whatever direction, you'll come to find that home is the most comfortable place to be.
but I am me - East is East, a continuation of the previous proverb reference, and hard-hitting 1999 British Comedy film.

77.
pull the ropes! The sails tear quick - slack in the rope.
cut some me, the job's not bad - to cut someone some slack.
all that's me's picked up, just be glad - to pick up the slack.
enough, I'm tired, ah-hum, it's that time already? Well I, cough, I'm off - to slack off.

78.
I'm cut but know that is the best, the newest - to be cutting edge.
end of where I rest, I perch and anxious listen from my seat - to be on the edge of one's seat.
you have a me so have them beat - to have an edge on someone.
the drum and clap, I'm at an end of there append - appendage, the suffix *age* here is often pronounced identically to *edge*, as well as being on the edge of the word as indeed a suffix ought.

79.
it's all gone bad to me it's come - to go south, to deteriorate or decline.
and with the birds and their humdrum I'm warmer though it more depends - birds fly south for the winter, as referenced in riddle 73.

and by-and-by I'm only I because of how the paper lies - according to modern maps, north is north and south is south. But there is no reason why north shouldn't have been south and south couldn't have been north. The first Chinese compasses were referred to as south-pointing stones, but since the North Star was the main celestial navigational point for the northern hemisphere, north became the point of normality.

80.
I'm guilty though I did no wrong - a guilt trip.
when I was up, I'd fallen strong, you grazed the surface, scarred quite drastic - to trip up.
I'm the light you lost fantastic - trip the light fantastic, a humorous phrase meaning to dance nimbly, taken from Milton's poem *L'Allegro*;

Com, and trip it as ye go,
On the light fantastick toe.

taken down a path of words; story, that's me of memory - to take a trip down memory lane.

81.
of glass or chequered high glass stacks of thirty holy Mary's axe - 30 St. Mary Axe, London is the address and official name of the Gherkin. The Gherkin is a commercial skyscraper in the City of London, and a piece of iconic contemporary architecture.
oh dear, good gosh, rhymes absentee; I'm in a pretty family - to be in a pretty pickle or in trouble. Indeed gherkin doesn't rhyme with many things, and creating a couplet with a firkin, a small wooden keg or unit equal to 9 imperial gallons, is a challenge.

82.
just close your eyes and think of me - close your eyes and think of England is an expression which means to just get on and do something whether you want to or not, with a higher purpose in mind, like one's country. Often used comically and in reference to 'caressing' someone who's 'face is not worth sunburning', as Shakespeare might put it (Henry V).
of ancient feet and burning bows - 'And did those feet in ancient time' is a short poem by William Blake, best known for the adaptation into Jerusalem, an anthem and iconic song of England, once proposed by King George V to replace God Save the Queen (King at the time) as the national anthem.
and rowers go, smart sweat on hands, they band - a reference to the Oxford and Cambridge University annual boat race, which is so well known in the UK that is is simply refered to as The Boat Race.
to seas of angles land - angleland - England literally means 'the land of angles'.

83.
I'm all, I'm yours, so take my pearl - the world is your oyster.
I'm given to you, every girl and boy - to give someone the world.
every girl and boy will know you told me so - to tell the world, meaning to tell something to everyone.
though not enough? I'm double! Oh - The World is Not Enough, the theme song to the James Bond movie of the same name. James Bond being a fictional British Secret Service agent created by Ian Fleming, otherwise know as 007, read double-oh-seven, all agents of the story being referred to as double-ohs.
my difference is but everything - a world of difference, entirely different.
claw cling, you're on me; king - to be on top of the world.

84.
go me, pet shops to other lands - Go West, a song that found fame through the English band Petshop Boys, though was a cover of the American group Village People.
my life sings popular in bands - on the same musical theme, Westlife is a famous Irish pop band originally signed by Simon Cowell and managed by Louis Walsh, both to later become X Factor judges, The X Factor being a British television music competition founded by Simon Cowell that found popularity worldwide in various adaptations.
of men with holsters, hats and guns that ride into the setting sun - a western movie.
that sets right here so don't ride far - the sun sets in the west.
or else you'll miss just where you are - most readers of this book will more-than-likely be in western countries, where the native language is more likely to be English.

85.
the sum of me the same though long or short - a day is invariably 24 hours, though we say it has been 'a long day'.
won't give my time to those your sort - won't give someone the time of day.
my me you made - to make someone's day.

86.
I'm done to many things, how queer - how odd, how strange that things bend. This is also an indirect reference to the use of the term to describe homosexuality, along with the more recent slang of bent. Both terms are generally considered offensive, as they imply something perverse, though also and preferably imply difference and eccentricity.
backwards and over that one's ear - to bend over backwards, and to bend someone's ear, are both common idioms.
to rules and laws that govern lands - to bend the rules or law.
in futures may those falling sands be me-d - to bend the hands of

time, time often being depicted as sand in a hourglass.
and out of shape - to bend someone out of shape.
insane; to sylums bound the me-go-round - to go round the bend or go insane.

87.
your troubles seemed so far to be recalled - 'Yesterday, all my troubles seemed so far away', is the opening and iconic line of the Beatles song *Yesterday*.
recalled, cryptic, mixed; stay reedy - stay reedy is an anagram of yesterday.
not dim, not born to me, you're in your prime - to be, or not to be, born yesterday.
a ye olde time - yester day, refers to the archaic form of yester defining something last past. Yesterday is a compound noun.

88.
I'm hard - hard work or to be hard at work.
so try to make me light - to make light work of something.
and grunt, I'm tiring - grunt work.
don't bark but like a dog and not the lark - to work like a dog, as dogs work very hard. But don't lark around, as larks, well, are apparently far more carefree creatures. Another possible original to this expression does not derive from the skylark but from the old Yorkshire dialect word for lake, meaning 'to amuse oneself'.
around I'll stay until I'm done, the battle beat; I'm like a treat - to work like a treat.

90.
but on me, left to crowds anon - to be on the bench, a sporting reference.
you judge your progress on my back, my legs stand stark, so hark, I set my mark - to set a benchmark.

91.
you know the joke and I was there, what's monotone and coloured? Stare a moment - a well-known riddle or conundrum describing a newspaper; 'what's black and white and read all over?' As the riddle works on the pun of the word 'read' and the implication of the colour 'red', it loses its poignancy when written.
see my woven arts; I'm like the onion, many parts - The Onion is a popular American farcical digital newspaper.
I break but stay the same across - to break the news.

92.
so here I am, the next I'm gone - to be here today, gone tomorrow.
a con to think to live as I, the moment be - to live in the present, in the moment, in today.
to now I'm me - to this day, I'm today.

93.
I am, though act as if I'm not - to act like there's no tomorrow.
so let us eat, drink merrily, and why? For me we die - eat, drink, and be merry, for tomorrow we die, a common expression meaning to live life to its fullest, as opposed to the tone of riddle 92. The expression is actually a conflation of two biblical passages, as Isaiah states, 'let us eat and drink; for tomorrow we shall die', and Ecclesiastes has a similar sentiment though with less death and more merriment.

94.
first I am tender, seeming tripe - to be at a tender age, or to be young.
but grow until I'm good and ripe - to live to a ripe old age.
now pretty people follow and - age before beauty.
I act dependent on my stand - to act one's age.

95.

96.
bakers six-point-five the dozen - a dozen is twelve, but a baker's dozen is thirteen. So half of a baker's dozen is six-point-five. There are a few theories for a baker's dozen, but one of the best, if not for only its gruesomeness, basically states that bakers would give thirteen loaves for every twelve ordered to not to be seen as cheating their patrons. When making bread by hand, it was quite easy to not make the appropriate amount of loaves by weight of wheat corn, and throughout history there have been quite harsh punishments for miserly bakers, including the loss of hands from ancient Babylon to mid-13th century Britain.
more a distant kind of cousin - a half-cousin.
see then how my other lives - to see how the other half lives.
as with my heart dull efforts give - to do something half-heartedly.
for you've but heard a part, a wee bit that's not even me - that's not the half of it.

97.
you take me off or put me on - to put years on or take years off someone, different styles and looks can make someone appear old or younger than they might actually be.
in donkey's measured and aghast - in donkey's years, for a long time.
I'm light, so far I sure move fast - a light year, actually a measurement of distance. It measures the distance light can travel in a vacuum over one Julian calendar year.
don't run, won't skip or jump a heap, but sometimes leap - a leap year.

98.
hop to it, though I'm short a jump - hop, skip, jump, or triple jump, is a track and field event.
jump rope me in - jump rope is the American equivalent of

skipping rope in Britain.
loaf me a step bump - to skip a step or skip something. Bump also means to remove something and to loaf means to be lazy, both also suggesting not dong a full and proper job.
the class, I'm out - to skip a class.
I'm out now lost the chance - to skip out on something.
so startled, starts your heart and happy feet; do me a beat - one's heart skips a beat.

99.
before the face, my little friend - a buddy.
the best as if from the same pod - best buds, or best friends, like two peas in a pod.
and see that trouble's coming, with a snip, give it a nip - to nip something in the bud.

100.
think hard, I'll me to mind - something springs to mind.
and forever hope you will find - hope springs eternal.
and I'll to life - to spring to life.
no chicken crèche - to be no spring chicken.
in bed I spiral up and push, push off that lazy sheet; from me to feet - to spring to one's feet. Spiralling up in the bed are also bed springs.

101.
the Swallow, though I am not made - one swallow does not a summer make. As swallows are migratory they return to their normal grounds at the beginning of summer, the quote is taken from a remark by Aristotle, 'one swallow does not a summer make, nor one fine day; similarly one day or brief time of happiness does not make a person entirely happy'.
and dab the beads of sweat down foreheads run, an Indian pun - an Indian summer, an unseasonably dry and warm period, usually in autumn.

102.
I come with games - fun and games.
stay while they last - it was fun while it lasted.
tie down your clocks I'll move them fast - time flies when you're having fun.
have me make someone else's, point it's all in jest don't get disjointed - to make fun of someone.
just for me - something is just for fun.
not cups nor boxes, drums; in barrels come - a barrel of fun.

103.
it comes from me - something stems from something else.
it comes from me, I mean it comes to stern though never cold or glum, but to the back, across the ship - from stem to stern, or from front to back. The expression describes the full length of a ship. The passage continues with sailing imagery.
and crashes, beating on the waves, such ride; I'm here to stop the tide - to stem the tide of something, or to stop the course of a tendency.

104.
and tap my sweetheart rivers, eh, that waffle on all day - eh is a common Canadian interjection used in speech to confirm that the listener is indeed listening. Used naturally as an implicit request for back-channeling. Maple from maple trees is associated with Canada, and with topping waffles.

105.

You're Here

You're here, though not by your intent.
You came but wish you'd sooner went.
Your name is all that holds you back
Or silence where your name does lack

A cord, a string, the puppeteer
Has deemed it so that you wait, here
You haven't budged an inch,
You haven't twitched or squirmed or flinched
A muscle, beads of sweat drip down
In waves that fill your mouth, you drown
In time that doesn't cease but stands until
You like the time stand still
And listen to the ticking clock,
Each tick, each tock, a noxious mocking
Chime that turns your stomach more,
Though not your stomach you're here for
An endless stream of people fill
And leave again the room sits still
Can't enter, for the doors are barred,
Lay bare your chest if torn now scarred,
If cut now scabbed, where hit a bruise,
Where pain; now all sensation lose
The breath you had, your life to kill,
To quench yet remains with you still
A syllable is all you need,
With God you deal, Devil plead
To sound the name you hear all day,
From lips of those that know you say
So often trumpets to a drill
A march that's not marched this way still
You're here, though not by your intent.
You came but wish you'd sooner went.
Your name is all that holds you back
Or silence where your name does lack.
While everything is busy and it seems all disappear;
Inevitably, you're still here.

106.
across the battered shores I topple; fall, but here I stand a longer name to call - across the Atlantic Ocean, in American English the season commonly known as 'fall'.
fill your holes and through my blankets rustle - to stock for the winter, like animals collecting nuts, running through the blankets of fallen leaves.
soon you'll sleep and in your homes you'll dine; your years of mine - one's Autumn years, or later years of life.

107.
to have or take me - to have or take a seat.
to have or take me at the edge; and anxiously - to be at the edge of one's seat or to be excited or nervous due to uncertainty.
but not sure, pressure's building, you're in what? You've lost the plot; I'm hot - to be in the hot seat.

108.
if your thoughts have gone and lost their me, you're left empty - to lose a train of thought.

109.
so through your mind I am a blink - something flashes through one's mind.
and in the pan, a short-lived star - to be a flash in the pan, describes any short-lived effort that dies in the attempt. The expression is often used to describe one-hit wonders, or celebrity stars that become famous for a very short time.
recall the embers burning, wrack, retrace my track; I'm back - to have a flashback.

110.
I'm coming so you best be ready - 'Winter is coming' is the motto of the House Stark in the popular book and television series Game of Thrones.
I also bring my wonderland, where angels sing - 'Winter Wonderland' is a popular winter song written in 1934 and since then has been covered by over 200 artists. Winter Wonderland is also the name of the seasonal winter fair held in London's Hyde Park, a Royal Park and one of the largest in London.
and on the top a thin veiled thread that covers all as brides are wed - to be snow-topped or to have a layer of snow settle.
but in the middle; I am dead - in the dead of winter, in the middle of winter when it's most cold and dark.

111.
if lucky laugh, if not then cry, but either way to me they fly - to laugh or cry all the way to the bank.
me on something; you count on that - to bank on something.
buy one for two and give a tip as token; for I'm broken - to break the bank or to use up all of one's money. The expression possibly derives from the rare occurrence in casino gambling when a gambler wins more money than the house has on hand.

112.
I'm easy as from duck to do - to be as easy as duck soup, a familiar saying possibly first published in a Detroit newspaper in 1893 referring to those being conned as 'duck soup'.
we're thick as peas - to be as thick as pea soup.
but do me up - to be souped up, or modified and enhanced.
in thick or thin, in trouble slip, it's me you're in - to be in the soup, or in trouble.

113.
that's everything but in me sinks, that's everything of which you'll think - everything but the kitchen sink, or everything one can think of.
so if it's hot don't scream or shout, don't pout; you best get out - if you can't stand the heat, get out of the kitchen.

114.
you know you've got a me, on it - to have a handle on something, to have control.
a little fragile me, with care - to handle something with care.
I help you go but now all's gone awry; jump from me, off you fly - to fly off the handle, or to lose one's temper. The expression was first found in print in 'The Attaché; or, Sam Slick in England' written by Thomas C. Haliburton. When speaking of an axe-head coming lose from the handle uncontrollably, Haliburton said, 'He flies of the handle for nothing'. Haliburton also coined the phrases 'ginger up', and 'won't take no for an answer'.

115.
all's gone wrong, too late perhaps too early; take an early me - to take a bath or an early bath, to stop doing an action earlier than planned, or to possibly give up or have been knocked out of some planned competition.

116.
there's none like me so from me start - there's no place like home, the famous line repeated by Dorothy in L. Frank Baum's The Wonderful Wizard of Oz, though the line is far older, for instance J. K. Paulding's The Backwoodsman (1818), reads, 'What'er may happen, wheresoe'er we roam, However homely, still there's naught like home'.
I'm where you stay and leave your heart - home is where the heart is.
and with the cows at dusk, come back - till the cows come home.
and at me, make yourself a snack - to make oneself or feel at home.
you cut, you mix and knead, you know what's in it as the butter's weighed; I'm made - to be homemade.

117.
my mouth profane takes lucky shots in French, though not a French word taught - to speak French or to mind one's French, to speak profanely, or to have a potty mouth.
takes lucky shots - to take a pot shot. The first known use of the term potshot is in 1843 delineating a shot taken that is unsporting but whose only objective is to provide food to fill a cooking pot.
you ought not look, I'm rather shy, you'll stick me on standby - a watched pot never boils.

118.
I celebrate your baby born, your wedding day with gifts adorn - a baby or bridal shower.
the brisk winds howl about my risk - to have a risk of showers, or rainfall.

119.
it's ready, fresh, it just came off - to be straight off the shelf.
not perfect but too fair to scoff - products off the shelf are typi-

cally of lower quality than custom made products, but more reasonably priced.
too difficult decisions are, too tough to yet agree; put it on me - to put something on the shelf, or leave it for a moment to return to later.

120.
let's talk me while work is good - to talk shop.
I'll chop, so first let's pop the hood - a chop-shop, a place where stolen cars are taken apart to be sold.
they set me up! I think you'll find - to set up shop, or to open shop.
you're safe, don't worry, I'll not force or threat; don't sweat - a sweatshop.

121.
all shapely liquors I anoint - a church key, a tool used to open bottle tops.
if you hold me, all points assess, I'm sure I'll lead you to success - to hold the key to success.
less I'm on you with golden locks - to be kept under lock and key, just as the famous tale of Rapunzel. Rapunzel, a German fairy tale assembled by the Brother's Grimm, tells of a young lady with long golden hair kept locked in a tower by a witch.

122.
and nailed to a grand old mast - to nail one's colours to the mast. The expression probably dates back to a specific naval battle in 1797 between the English and Dutch. At the time, to lower one's flag, or colours, meant surrender. The flagship of the English fleet, the Venerable, was engaged and had the mainmast and flag struck down. The remaining fleet might have interpreted this to mean they should surrender. So a young sailor, Jack Crawford, climbed the mast and nailed the flag where the rest of the fleet could see. The English fleet

137

won the battle, which was seen as the turning point of when the Dutch began to lose dominance of the seas and the British took control.
so cast not under false across the blue - to sail under false colours.
but show one's true - to show one's true colours.

123.
sometimes I roll up high, down fast, make little children cry, downcast - a roller coaster.
downcast, resigned to me, through life - to coast through life.
and, lo! Along the seaside go - to go along the coast, to be a coaster.

124.
tap my face and enter me - to tap the enter key on the keyboard. The first four lines include a mix of different keyboard keys; enter, space, one, two, three, shift, Q, U.
you'll need a plank of locks - the purpose of a key board must surely be to address a plank of locks.

125.
one like what checks your hunger, though - a bite.
the other makes sweet serum flow - a bee, or B.
an starts the second, first an a - an MB, a megabyte.

126.
drop me, I'm under, hidden that - to drop one's drawers, or drop one's underpants.
I'm simple; store don't create, not the smartest; plethora of artists - a set of drawers.

127.
It has my blood and lies on rocks, a sentry like the sky - to have blue blood, to be blue-blooded.

and talks of dull and downcast things it weeps - to be blue, or depressed.
up death has come and to the screen - the blue screen of death, an error screen displayed on a Windows computer after a fatal system error, or system crash.
the devil and my sea between - to be between the devil and the deep blue sea. There are many theories to the origin of this expression, though the most interesting is of the seam of a ship. From bow to stern runs the seam often called the devil. When the seam had to be sealed, or caulked, to stop water from entering the ship, a sailor would be levied down in a bosun's chair, or boatswain's chair, a type of rope harness. The sailors would then be between the devil, and the deep blue sea, and in a rather perilous position.

128.
eat me though I'm light, not air - iron as a dietary source is essential to all body cells. Primarily, iron acts as a carrier of oxygen.
so pump by choice your body tears - to pump iron, or work out. Working out, in effect, tears muscles fibres. The resistance training causes trauma to the muscle fibres that encourages satellite cells to repair or replace damaged muscle fibre, leading to an increase in the cross-sectional area, or hypertrophy.
and strike, you see I'm hot and bother - to strike while the iron is hot.
do with my fist see them follow you - to rule with an iron fist.
as I'm a super man - Iron Man, Tony Stark, is a fictional super hero from the Marvel world of comic books. Though he is a super hero, he is an ordinary man, or at least an eccentric ingenious engineer. Superman, Kal-El, on the other hand, is from the DC Comics universe, and has his own array of super powers.

129.
All reference playing cards. *Four times to ten* are the four suits in the deck with cards up to ten. The *full attentive court* refers to the picture cards. *The royal couple* are the king and queen, while the *knave or knight* are terms to describe what is now more commonly called the Jack. The Knave had to adopt a new name as the initial K had already been adopted by the king. However, the term jack was first seen as a lower class term as demonstrated in Charles Dickens' Great Expectations, 'He calls the knaves, jacks, this boy!'

130.
and make me as you do to prove your effort, no one doubts that from the sound - to make a racket, or to make a loud sound. Also, many tennis players in their efforts 'grunt' in their swing.
make fast what's round - what's round is the tennis ball, made to move quickly.

131.
it's just not right, not fair, get in a me and dance with ruffled hair - to get into a song and dance about something.
and feathers as a swan, my last big work and then I'm gone - a swan song, the last, big work or performance of an artist.
don't drill or dig, but break, or quickly first into me burst - to burst into song.

132.
I count your days, the end is near - for one's days to be numbered.
I'm crunched and see that's it I fear - a number cruncher, to crunch the numbers.
that any me of things could come - to be any number of things.
I'm up but no need to be glum - one's number is up.
as one, a public enemy - public enemy number one.
but safety in a group of me - there is safety in numbers.

133.
it's light, but is it light as I? - to be as light as a feather.
a mass of me that flies together all the same we strain - birds of a feather flock together.
but slow and dull if in your brain - to be feather brained.
but in a hat, be proud of that! Stand tall - to have or be a feather in one's cap.
sleep well in bed; I'm underhead - a feather pillow.

134.
I'm black and white and red, or as it goes - a hint also used in riddle 91, referring to the joke 'what's black and white and read all over?' Crosswords appear in newspapers, also printed in black and white.
though many, seems I'm often run an angry one - a cross word.

135.
as legendary death I bring - the ace of spades in folklore is known as the death card. Though it is unclear why, the folklore is quite well known, which incited a slew of cases where gangsters in the 1930s and then American soldiers in the Vietnam War left the cards on the bodies of their enemies.
me, hold the line with all the same, we'll rule - to hold all the aces.
we'll rule the bridge and hold 'em, game is fixed - bridge, or contact bridge, is one of the most popular playing card games around the world, even having its own governing body, the World Bridge Federation. Hold 'em or Texas holdem is a variation of standard poker, one of the world's most popular gambling card games. One source puts Texas holdem as second and bridge as forth on a list of the top 10 popular card games.
is fixed, and I'm called what I'm called - to call a spade a spade.

136.
as if you wear an Eastern shawl - like a hijab, a veil that covers the head and chest of Muslim women, making them appear more like silhouettes.

137.
you paid as if they'd captured me - to pay a king's ransom.
the most, which is quite fittingly - fit for a king, and a king's portion is of course the most.
the tallest turret, hill or…stop! - the king of the castle, or king of the hill.
you ape, it's not for you but mind don't hurl! Gently! The girl! - King Kong, the fictional colossal gorilla, conceived and created by American filmmaker Merian C. Cooper.

138.
three-hundred soldiers on my hand - there are three hundred marks on a typical 30cm ruler, to indicate each mm.

139.
that's one in twelve, like other men - to be a dime a dozen, common and just like everyone else.
fact: half of me is silver-white - a nickel.
and with it I'm a common blight - to be nickle-and-dime, also meaning ordinary and common.
er, no, how inappropriate a gripe; should speak in stars and stripes - the riddle is on the currency of the USA, but 'blighter', or the use of the term 'blight' to describe people, is British English and so inappropriate here. Best stick to stars and stripes, or American English.

140.
to the beat as on parade, but off and see their steps unmade - to be on key or to be off key, which was never a question.
when high the climax verberates a secret show? Then low - to

keep something low-key, secret or undisclosed.

141.
most valuable in me is seen - the jewel in the crown, or the most valuable thing amongst others.
uneasy lies this noble prop - uneasy lies the head that wears a crown, those with the most responsibilities are often more troubled, from Shakespeare's Henry IV.
and when he fell and tumbled down, in water soaked; I broke - 'Jack fell down and broke his crown', from the traditional English nursery rhyme 'Jack and Jill'. The rhyme is considered nonsense verse, primarily because one does not go up a hill to fetch water, but down to the well.

142.
I'm square, four corners, though three-de - a reference to cushions being neither square nor cube, but three-dimensional squares.
take from another one a pin - a pin cushion.
and stitch me up again, I'm tattered though; I'll take the blow - to cushion the blow.

143.
I'm friendly, I'm for love extended - an engagement ring. Diamonds have been associated with engagement rings in the US and around the world for three-quarters of a century now, all thanks to a marketing campaign by De Beers. Slogans like 'A Diamond is Forever', considered the number one slogan of the century in 1999, and the 'two months salary rule' pushed a dying market into a psychology standard.
surely we'd half be best friended - diamonds are a girl's best friend.
did this street rat win the scruff? I live in sands and in the rough - a diamond in the rough, you cannot see the true beauty of a rough diamond before cutting. Disney used the terms street

rat and a diamond in the rough to describe Aladdin in their movie of the same name.
I'm hard, cut me? You tickle, impish elf; I'll cut myself - the theory is that only a diamond can truly cut another diamond. Tools are diamond tipped, or diamond 'dusted', and used to cut along tetrahedral planes, where the diamond is structurally weakest.

144.
my English is most proper, so - the Queen's English.
won't drag, dress well, you get the gist - a drag queen.
behave as well I should then rest the state - my head - the Queen is head of state.
where I've the biggest bed - queen sized beds in the UK are the biggest. Though there seems to be much disparity not only internationally in bed sizes, but also domestically in the correct terminology, many people in the UK refer to Super-King sized beds as Queen sized beds.

145.
at penny-pinching partners throw - in Bleak House, one of Charles Dickens' major novels, there is a well-known scene where, as Mrs Smallweed yells crazed about money, Mr Smallweed throws a cushion at her, making himself fall over in the process.
for I will I the blow - to cushion the blow, also the final clue of riddle 142 of the same answer.

146.

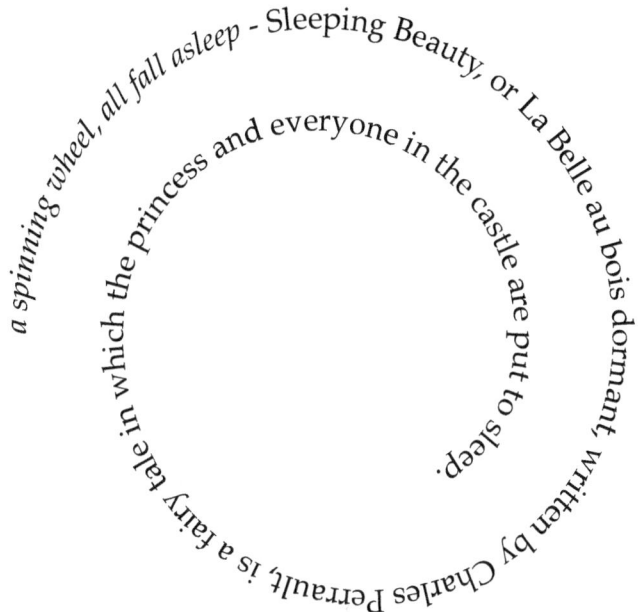

a spinning wheel, all fall asleep - Sleeping Beauty, or La Belle au bois dormant, written by Charles Perrault, is a fairy tale in which the princess and everyone in the castle are put to sleep.

in clouds I'm built, though dreams unseen - to build castles in the sky, or to make equally impossible plans.
I own a king, speak not of queens - the king of the castle.
when all about me water flows - a castle moat.

147.

148.
declare what must be done be done - to declare war.
with waving flags begin the act - an act of war, not a theatrical act as is implied.
get out you sheep, you drone, you white faced clone - the Clone Wars, is an event in the movie series Star Wars and an animated microseries. Each clone wears the same white armour and white helmet. The use of the term drone is also a reference to the unmanned aircraft in the Star Wars series.
this is my zone - a war zone.

149.
a young Boleyn - Anne Boleyn was the second wife of Henry VIII, Queen of England, and in order to wed young Boleyn, the reason why King Henry VIII broke from the Catholic Church. She must have been quite a beauty. However, not all accounts agree on the matter as the Venetian diplomat Francesco Sanuto described Anne as 'not one of the handsomest women in the world; she is of middling stature, swarthy complexion, long neck, wide mouth, a bosom not much raised and eyes which are black and beautiful'.
a web-like pattern delicate that buffs around your scruff - a neck lace. Scruff refers to the scruff of one's neck.

150.
no hole, yet in me you go down - to go down in defeat.
they came and saw, then went to town - 'veni, vidi, vici', a Latin phrase often attributed to Julius Caesar meaning, 'I came, I saw, I conquered'.
they took your king, check! Toppled queen - a defeat in the game of chess.
I'm bitter, from my jaws a batch of not me they did snatch - to snatch victory from the jaws of defeat.

151.
my money's gone mysterious - a fool and his money are soon parted.
'we don't know how!' the adults say, though I know they do love to play me - to play the fool or to pretend to not know something.
me and the children tell the truth, no spoof - children and fools tell the truth, an old proverb.
this is my proof - to be fool proof.

152.
you made your own, now it's too late - to dig one's own grave.
take it to me, a secret plot - to take something to one's grave, to keep something a secret.
so in me over turn - to turn, or turn over, in one's grave.

153.
and held to someone high or low, about the holder more I show - to hold a candle to someone, to measure oneself up to someone.
and when you're tired, life takes toll, I tend to work both ends - to burn the candle at both ends.

154.
main entry is an answer; key, a guff, remark, retort or plea - 'key', 'guff', 'remark', 'retort', 'plea', and at the end of the riddle, 'reply' are all synonyms of 'answer'.
anti-what-you-call a question - the word 'question' is an antonym of 'answer'.
actually a dinosaur of articles am I - a the saurus.

155.
me my opinion at the top - to voice one's opinion, and to say something at the top of one's voice.
together I am stronger, stop - the collective voice.
stop and lower or you all can raise, me - to lower or raise one's voice.
me, throw me, what a haze - to throw one's voice.

156.
come catch me, though it's not a hunt - to catch a ride.
so cry a weapon, climb in front - to ride shotgun.
you're inside though said to be on - to be on a ride.
prepare you fool, I might be quite bumpy - a bumpy ride.
you're taken for a me - to take someone, or for someone to be taken, for a ride.

157.
me me on as it might be rough - to strap me on, or strap on a strap.
I'm where you are when sat not still - when sat in a moving vehicle.
stop you go through the window, sill a beam but softer - a sill is horizon timber forming framework to support a structure, much as a strap supports, though the strap may be horizontal or diagonal.
I clad this me-ing lad - a strapping (young) lad.

158.
lift up your hand, fingers erect - to make the V sign. Recommended by Victor de Laveleye, former Belgian Minister of Justice and director in the BBC, as an emblem of victory against occupying forces during World War II. Gaining popularity across Europe, on the 19th of July 1941, Prime Minister Winston Churchill gave a speech approving the message and began using the gesture regularly. Interestingly, the sign become so prevalent that instead of trying to remove it, the German forces tried to adopt it to symbolise their victories against the allied forces. US President Richard Nixon used the sign for victory in the Vietnam War, leading to anti-war activists to redefine the gesture as a symbol of peace, which then spread to Japan, where people of all ages have decided it necessary to declare peace in every photograph they take.
and though a pretty penny never paid, a sacrifice came at what price? - victory came at what price?

159.
it's penguins dance the longest word we sing - Mary Poppins, the 1964 musical Fantasy film involved a scene of dancing penguins, the nonsense word 'supercalifragilisticexpialidocious', and a famous scene on a merry-go-round.
a happy moving ring - a merry-go-round.

160.
stamp, one and two, within your heart - a heartbeat.
trop trample, but the horse is dead - to beat a dead horse.
the birds are in the bush instead! Grab sticks and guns and see them, hit - to beat around the bush, British gamekeepers would hire beaters that would swing sticks around the bushes to flush out game such as pheasants for shooting.
there's one and two, so quit! Me it! - beat it! Get out of here! Also the title of Grammy Award winning Michael Jackson record.

161.
a weaker pen - with sword, as the pen is mightier than the sword.
or parker nib - or with arrow, as the Parker Pen Company logo is an arrow, depicted on each pen nib.
forget me not! Take back your words, breathe in each lung, for I'm unsung - an unsung hero.

162.
I'm given up? - to give up hope.
find the last me - the last hope.
the Ant, who took me high into the sky - from the song *High Hopes*, first popularised by Frank Sinatra. *High Hopes* won Best Original Song at the 32nd Academy Awards for its introductory appearance in the 1959 film *A Hole in the Head*.
your heart is cross, concludes I die - to cross my heart and hope to die.
I must be good, be bound to heaven, well I'm not in hell - there's not a hope in hell.

163.
I'm played though not all players know - to play a joke on someone.
inside and most are clueless, though - an inside joke.

aside sometimes beneath me there's a poignant mark on real affairs
- all jokes aside.
and though I'm never cleaned, please don't get shirty, only sometimes dirty - a dirty joke.

164.
a long I plod - to have clown feet, or long feet.
and me around - to clown around, or not be serious.
From fear you go; I am cool, row! - Coulrophobia, a fear of clowns.

165.
agreeable to your ears me - to be music to one's ears.
but now's the time to stand your place, so moment brace and to me face - to face the music.

166.
I am the same to the whole sum, the loaf of bread or just a crumb - which is heavier, a pound of feathers or a pound of lead? The famous riddle in which one might fall for the naïve answer, though a pound of anything is still a pound.
waves lash on pebbles - here, lash is a synonym for pound.
pebbles where I fit - pebbles, or stone and pounds are measures of weight. If one is overweight, one cannot fit. Pebbles being small stones, can fit. A small and very obscure hint, so give yourself a pat on the back if you got it.
I'm fine, not sterling I'll admit - pound sterling, the currency of the UK. The term probably comes from Middle English *steorra+ling*, or star-ling, because some Norman pennies carried a small star.
I'm wrote and read quite different fashions – lb is read pound. Lb is actually an abbreviation of the Latin word libra. Libra is both the astrological sign depicted with scales, and also the ancient Roman unit of measure, libra pondo. The term pound conversely comes from the latter part of the ancient

Roman unit.
note, most want to lose my rations - to lose pounds.

167.
I'm over you so watch my steps - to be taken under someone's wings.
pray on on me, I'll raise your rep-utation - on a wing and a prayer.
and beat the nothing, find me clipped - clipped wings.
and though you're not prepared, don't up and quit; me it - to wing it.

168.
I'm of good health - to be a picture of good health.
I sure am pretty - as pretty as a picture.
stand for you, lie land or city - portrait pictures are standing taller than they are wide, while landscape and cityscapes are lying, wider than they are tall.
strokes describe what happened true - to paint a picture, with paint strokes, or to describe what happened vividly.
as I'm a tad more perfect you - to be picture perfect.
my value fills 'bout quarter a short story - a picture is worth a thousand words. One source puts flash fiction at under 1,000 words, short stories at 1,000-7,500 words, novelettes at 7,500-20,000 words, novella at 20,000-50,000 words and novels at over 50,000 words, though there are really no hard and fast rules.
frig I'm big! - the big picture.

169.
no feathers and I'm not a bird - though the dragon is a mythology creature, it is typically depicted with serpentine or reptilian traits.
oh fools that chase me, empty men - to chase the dragon, or to smoke heroin is a phrase of Cantonese origin from Hong

Kong.
I'm waiting in my den - Dragon's Den is the UK, and a best known, name for a reality television programme, referred to as Shark Tank in the US, that spread around the world. The programme originated in Japan where it was called Money Tigers.

170.
don't look and rule - don't judge a book by its cover.
I'm open, upright - to be an open book.
I am used for all the tricks in me, some underhanded stealth - to use every trick in the book.
play by myself - to play by the book.

171.
you get me not by choice, and shout - to get a fright.
with each step through the set, each stage - to have stage fright.
don't burn your house to me the mouse let be - burn not your house to fright the mouse away, a proverb meaning don't drastically disturb something which needn't be, or don't overreact.

172.
from duck's off south I'm off and see - like water off a duck's back.
I lost my fish and hence distress - like a fish out of water.
this is my world, the Mariner's as well - 'the Mariner' is a reference to *Waterworld*, the 1995 action-adventure movie in which a mutated Mariner tries to survive the harsh realities of a world covered entirely by water.
for here I come, if not comes hell - come hell or high water.

173.
while chasing down the sun I blot - it's raining cats and dogs.
and eating, then I'm mostly hot - a hot dog.

I'm sleeping here, so let me lay - let sleeping dogs lie.
for I will have my day - every dog has its day.

174.
I someone over, awe's amount - to be bowled over, or surprised an in awe of something.
and life would be a better me, if just full of cherry - life is a bowl of cherries.

175.
be me'd away and don a gown - to be spirited away, or to be concealed and snuck away. Also the Western title of the Japanese animated movie *Sen to Chihiro*, Oscar winner 2003 for best animated feature.
when happy, in me high and good - to be in high, or good, spirits.
and you and I, we're much the same, we're kin, we're meant to be - to be kindred spirits.
that's me! - that's the spirit!

176.
a foreign chicken missed the vet, collect from all the crowd a bet - the French word poule, meaning chicken or hen, is the origin for many English words including pony, poultry and pullet, and of course, some uses of the word pool. According to The Etymologicon by Mark Forsyth, the French had a game called jeu de la poule, in which they threw things at hens, from which the term poule became synonymous with the target, and then with the betting stake used, which was collected before the bout. Then finally association broadened to any collection, giving us carpool lanes, gene pools and anything that is pooled together.
now with a stick, don't swing but hit and see your colours down a pit - the snooker-like game of pool gets its name from the same source, as originally bets were pooled before each

game.
one box in which you all contain, no train but special lane - a car-pool lane.

177.
I'm wise and so they beat me, oh 'it's your own fault', they said 'you know' - a wise guy.
they're me but tough - a tough guy.
I take the fall - a fall guy.
I'm nice, but watch them pass, I'm not so fast so come in last - nice guys finish last.

178.
I'm big and rake the land, so dig straight moats, I'll long the side and pull the boats - the Romans introduced the use of mules to pull boats on their waterways in Britain. Such a practice continued for many years, with horse-drawn boats along the canal systems being the main mode of transport, driving the Industrial Revolution.
go to the water, take a drink, or nigh, I'll not - you can lead a horse to water, but you can't make it drink.
get off, I'm high! - get off you high horse!
I'm dark - a dark horse.

179.
if you see me I'm in your eye - beauty is in the eye of the beholder.
why not cut and dig, I'm not so deep - beauty is only skin deep.
though I'll come back when you're asleep - to get some beauty-sleep.
I dance with clocks and candle sticks and feast; and with the beast - Beauty and the Beast, or La Belle et la Bete, is a traditional French fairy tale written by Jeanne-Marie Leprince de Beaumont, later to be adapted by Disney into an animated film.

180.
quiet! As if in a church - to be quiet as a church mouse.
I lay my plans, they're half the best - the best laid schemes o' mice and men, a line from Robert Burns' poem To a Mouse, meaning that even the most carefully prepared plans can go awry. The poem is the source for the title of John Steinbeck's Of Mice and Men.
men take the mick, though meant in jest - to take the mick, or to tease someone is an example of Cockney rhyming slang. To take the piss, an expression of the same meaning, became to take the Mickey Bliss, and then to take the Mickey. Often erroneously attributed to Mickey Mouse.
I most explore on days all done - mice being primarily nocturnal come out when the days are done.

181.
you're caught by me, though never chased - to be caught by surprise.
I took you but 'twas I that braced - to be taken by surprise.

182.
I might be none, or two or three - just not one.
quote me a cyclops may have caught; me here, or not alone distraught - in Homer's epic poem, the *Odyssey*, when Odysseus found himself and his men trapped by the cyclops Polyphemus, he claimed his name was no one or nobody. When then they blinded the cyclops and he called for help, he called that nobody was harming him.
I know - no one knows.
I need to know - no one need know.
just go away, I'm home - no one's home.

183.
dare sheer my beard right where I laze? - to beard the lion in his den.

you take a slice but let's be fair, all the remaining is my share - the lions share.

184.
my smell a sweet me-drop to lick - a Pear drop is an old British sweet.
all's gone me shaped, so here's the trick - to go pear-shaped.
alone I face the air, though sister here and there, yet I'm a pair - pairs don't grow in bunches or in twos. The final line is a reference to the homophone of pear and pair.

185.
I give out fruit, or lead you there, I make you shamed to be so bare - the serpent, partly response for the fall of man.
and if you can't see when we pass, I'm in the grass - a snake in the grass, something that is sneaky, sly and dangerous.

186.
I me that - I fear that
you will rush as fools to where's untrod by Angel mules - fools rush in where Angels fear to tread.
but never me - never fear.
I'm owned by God, so put me in the quaking squad - to put the fear of God in someone.

187.
no fish with fins nor beasts with feet, before it all, these two did clash - God created the land and the water on the third day, before any birds or beasts existed. God created the animals on the fifth and sixth days to fill the land and water.
yet one without the other drops, up prop secure - to shore something up, to prop or support something up.
I'm sure - sure and shore are homophones.

188.
though not to nicks or find you're moved - to rub salt in a wound. A nick is a small cut on the surface or edge of something. Interestingly, in British English exists the expression in good nick, meaning in good condition. The origin of the phrase seems to be unclear, though why the same word would apply to a cut and to good condition is peculiar. Some suggest this usage originates from the application to racing horses and successful breeding. There is also a French slang expression c'est nickel of the same meaning, though which language borrowed from the other is also unclear.
become a natural grounded me - to be the salt of the earth, and also a reference to ground salt.
though waters filled quite contrary - salt water.
and don't believe it all, you're right to flinch, just take a pinch - to take something with a pinch of salt.

189.
not cold, I'm feeling! - a cold fish, or someone who is unfeeling.
miss the haul - if fish are caught, the collective terms are a catch, drought or haul.
as I remain in the same school - the most common collective noun for fish being school, though draft, nest and shoal are also acceptable and some academics argue that school is incorrect.
find plenty creatures in the sea, but not so many me - there are plenty of fish in the sea, an expression indicating the variety of possibilities one still has. Though, goldfish we associate more with pet shops, carnivals and home fish tanks than the open waters.

190.

191.
let's bring it out, it's shy and coy - to bring someone out of their shell.
but briefly, see the nut - in a nut shell.
not rocked explosions knocked; I'm shocked - to be shell shocked.

192.
I'm beautiful, though lost the plot - *A Beautiful Mind* is an excellent biographical film on the life of Nobel Laureate John Nash, starring Russell Crowe, which won four Academy Awards. In the story, Nash is diagnosed with paranoid schizophrenia.
I'm over it - mind over matter.
all kept together in one frame - to be in a certain frame of mind.
but change - to change one's mind.
so much I'm lost - to lose one's mind.

193.
I'm fruitful, breed when in the wild, captured, only man-made child - modern cultivation creates edible bananas that are seedless, or rather with seeds diminished to tiny black specks, however bananas in the wild do have seeds.
family is thought of wrong - botanically a banana is classed as a berry.

194.
so lined like colonel hath-I grunt - Colonel Hathi is a bull elephant and fictional character in Rudyard Kipling's *The Jungle Book*.
No soldier I, but taught a king, babar rarar I toot and sing - Babar the Elephant is King of the Elephants in Jean de Brunhoff's children's book *Histoire de Babar*.
and don't forget - an elephant never forgets.
I've two types be - African and Asian (Indian) elephants, African elephants being bigger and more wrinkled.

remember that like me - to have a memory like an elephant.

195.
mechanic faces - screens.
melted sand - glass is made from liquid sand, when sand, mostly silicon dioxide, is heated and melts at about 1700C (3090F).
you think like me on many things - to reflect on something.
to flect again I fling - to re-flect.

196.
I swim the sea, touch me beware! - it is a common superstition that if you touch a frog you get warts. The warts humans catch are in fact a human virus, however some of the wart-like bumps on frogs or toads can be dangerous, such as those behind the ears, which are parotoid glands and can contain poison.
but kiss and all your dreams come true - if you kiss a frog it will turn into a prince, a now common theme of fair tales derived from The Frog King, or Der Froschkonig oder der eiserne Heinrich, a German folk tale included in the Brother's Grimm collection.
I'm in your throat, you're turning blue - to have a frog in one's throat.
I'm big for this small place - to be a big frog in a small pond.

197.
though I've no legs, you'll find I walk - a walking stick.
they'll gawk, they scold, you'll get a lot of me - to get a lot of stick, an informal British expression meaning to be criticised or teased a lot.

198.
express me well - to express one's anger.
and manage it - anger is something we try to manage in a

clinical context. *Anger Management* is also the title of a popular Jack Nicholson and Adam Sandler movie on the topic.
not popular, though all the rage - to be all the rage, or severe anger.
beware you don't end in my cage - the cage of anger is a 'street' term for a prison.
I sizzle, make you change into a thistle, with me bristle - to bristle with anger.

199.
I'm near so jump and look around, I'm at you - to bark at someone.
madly doing found - to be barking mad.
you run and climb the wrong damn tree - to be barking up the wrong tree.
go take a break and grab a bite as, curse, you'll find me something worse - for one's bark to be worse than one's bite.

200.
I start quite small like insect, march - ant.
I see it coming - i c.
here it floats, a ripple of discordant notes - 'anticipation went through me like a ripple of discordant notes', A. E. Maxwell. Here Ann Maxwell describes anticipation as lacking harmony, but surely a clever reference to harmonic anticipation in music whereby a note is approached and then remains the same. Anticipation is a technique that allows one to anticipate a change in chord to create a sense of motion, far from being inharmonious.
I pat it on - ipation.
use tact; prevent it in me act - anticipation is an action taken to counteract or prevent something.

201.
this book has all of me - to have all the answers.
it vainly thinks to prayers it's come - to be the answer to someone's prayers.
me back? Don't quibble, sulk or slack - don't answer back.
but if you check so stupidly, you'll get a stupid me - ask a stupid question and you'll get a stupid answer.

Two birds within a stone's throw.

www.ingramcontent.com/pod-product-compliance
Lightning Source LLC
Chambersburg PA
CBHW071951070426
42453CB00012BA/2124